RELIGION AND PLACE

Liverpool's historic places of worship

Published by English Heritage, Kemble Drive, Swindon SN2 2GZ
www.english-heritage.org.uk
English Heritage is the Government's statutory adviser on all aspects of the historic environment.

Printing 10 9 8 7 6 5 4 3 2 1

First published 2008

ISBN 978 1 873592 88 5
Product code 51334

The Liverpool Culture Company has made a financial contribution towards the publication of this book.

British Library Cataloguing in Publication Data
A CIP catalogue record for this book is available from the British Library.

The National Monuments Record is the public archive of English Heritage. For more information, contact NMR Enquiry and Research Services, National Monuments Record Centre, Kemble Drive, Swindon SN2 2GZ; telephone (01793) 414600.

Front cover
The choir of Ullet Road Unitarian Church. [AA040397]

Inside front cover
The sumptuous lectern of St Dunstan's Church, Earle Road. [AA045392]

Back cover
A view through the buttress passage, the Lady Chapel of the Anglican Cathedral. [DP034204]

Photographs by Keith Buck, Mike Hesketh-Roberts, Tony Perry, Bob Skingle and Peter Williams.
Graphics by Allan T Adams.
Brought to publication by Rachel Howard and René Rodgers, Publishing, English Heritage.
Edited by Sara Peacock.
Page layout by Simon Borrough.
Printed in the UK by Cambridge Printing.

RELIGION AND PLACE

Liverpool's historic places of worship

Sarah Brown and Peter de Figueiredo

The City of Liverpool

Liverpool
EUROPEAN
CAPITAL OF CULTURE

ENGLISH HERITAGE

Contents

Frontispiece
The west doors, Ullet Road
Unitarian Church. [AA04031]

Acknowledgements

The authors would like to record their appreciation of assistance of friends and colleagues in the preparation of this book: Joseph Sharples and Richard Pollard of the Buildings of England; Glynn Marsden of Liverpool City Council; Sharman Kadish of Jewish Heritage UK; and Paul Barnwell, Malcolm Cooper, Colum Giles, Ian Goodall, Louise O'Brien and Henry Owen John, past and present colleagues in English Heritage. Gary Corbett of English Heritage provided invaluable assistance with fieldwork, while graphics were provided by Allan Adams and photography was undertaken by Keith Buck, Mike Hesketh-Roberts, Tony Perry, Bob Skingle and Peter Williams. The Bishop of Liverpool, the Right Reverend James Jones, has lent his support and has generously written a Foreword.

Assistance has also been unstintingly forthcoming from the staff of Liverpool Record Office and Library and from National Museums, Liverpool. We thank Liverpool Record Office for supplying Figs 25, 55, 57 and the images on p4 and p52 and we thank Mills Media Ltd for allowing us to use the latter image. We thank National Museums Liverpool for supplying Fig 45 (from the Walker Art Gallery) and Fig 50 (from the Merseyside Maritime Museum). The Courtauld Institute of Art supplied Fig 46 and Martin Stewart provided Fig 63.

A particular debt of thanks is owed to all those clergy, church wardens and custodians of buildings we have visited. They have welcomed us to their cherished buildings with great kindness, patience and hospitality, and our text has been improved thanks to the information they shared with us. Any errors contained herein are our own.

Foreword

It is not possible to understand the history and heritage of Liverpool fully without recognising and understanding how faith has shaped the contours of this great city.

The religious dimension of Liverpool literally dominates the skyline; the spiritual life of the community is written in the stones of the city's places of worship. Cathedrals, chapels, churches, mosques, synagogues and temples all tell the story of how faith has been a consistent thread in the tapestry that is Liverpool's heritage. Over the centuries, these historic buildings have provided sacred spaces where people have gathered to mark occasions of contemplation, celebration and sadness. Places of worship are repositories for the collective memories of the communities which they serve and come into their own at times of communal stress. During every crisis – wartime bombing, the Toxteth riots, the Hillsborough tragedy – Liverpool's faith buildings have been places of sanctuary and support.

Over the years populations have shifted and local economies have changed so that religious buildings which once served vibrant communities have found themselves 'at risk'. It is to the credit of English Heritage that they, on behalf of the wider public, have recognised the cultural and architectural importance of these buildings and how they function at the heart of the community. English Heritage works closely with local communities for the present and for future generations.

People continue to gather in these living, breathing buildings for rites of passage, community events and for that simple spiritual experience of contemplation and prayer. For Liverpool's people and its visitors alike, its places of worship are both sites of pilgrimage and historic places to explore and enjoy.

Every building tells a part of Liverpool's remarkable story, as this fascinating book reveals. Reading the walls, the windows, the memorials and the architecture of a religious building opens our eyes to a local history which has sometimes remained hidden through the years. It is in these places that people recover a sense of their own personal history and identity, and find a renewed pride in their roots and a new sense of hope for the future.

The Right Reverend James Jones, Bishop of Liverpool

CHAPTER 1

Cathedral city

In common with several other English cities, Liverpool has two cathedrals. Unlike other cities, however, they were not begun in the Middle Ages; both belong to the 20th century. And in no other city are the cathedrals such icons, on a par with its two football clubs in the affections of its citizens. These two great buildings (Fig 1) – the Anglican Cathedral Church of Christ perched on a rocky ridge above the city, and the Catholic Cathedral of Christ the King, sited on an equally magnificent site at the top of Mount Pleasant – are within sight of one another and their history is a summation of Liverpool's sometimes turbulent sectarian past. When plans for a Catholic cathedral on the present site were first conceived in 1928, there can be no doubt that Archbishop Richard Downey intended his metropolitan church to challenge the Anglican Cathedral already rising above the city's skyline. Even their names are similar. In the 1970s and 1980s the two buildings, linked by a street called Hope, became symbols of religious reconciliation in a city long rent by sectarian tension. They now share in the city's regeneration and revitalisation, after years of economic decline and social unrest. Both have recently implemented schemes to enhance their facilities for worshippers, pilgrims and visitors.

Liverpool has long called forth great architecture and its places of worship are no exception. This book seeks to tell Liverpool's story through these buildings which have done so much to define the character of the city's many neighbourhoods and suburbs. In the 18th and 19th centuries, the periods of Liverpool's greatest growth, some of its finest buildings were churches and chapels. The two Christian cathedrals have a Jewish counterpart in the Old Hebrew Congregation Synagogue in Princes Road. With its sumptuously decorated interior, it is one of the finest and most important of the so-called 'cathedral synagogues' of the later 19th century, and its small but devoted congregation is lovingly restoring it, securing its future for the next generation. Within sight of the synagogue are two other remarkable places of worship: the Greek Orthodox Church of St Nicholas and the former Welsh Presbyterian Church. Both buildings are of almost cathedral-like proportions and served prosperous minorities distinguished from their fellow citizens by both religious observance and linguistic distinctiveness.

Metalwork in the Lady Chapel of the Anglican Cathedral. [DP034203]

In contrast to these great set pieces are the everyday landscapes of Liverpool's suburbs. A leisurely walk within a few miles of the city centre takes in buildings that sum up so much that is characteristic of Liverpool and the history of its places of worship: the rivalry between Protestant and Catholic, the importance of architecture in defining and proclaiming religious allegiance, the rich mix of nationalities and religious traditions in a city whose wealth was founded on international trade, and even the desire to praise God in a mother tongue. While all of these places of worship attract smaller congregations than in the past, suffer from the drift of their communities out of the city centre, and face challenges in maintaining and preserving their historic fabric, all remain central to the life of the city and contribute to the extraordinary quality of Liverpool's architectural heritage.

Figure 1 *Cathedral city: Liverpool's two cathedrals seen from across the Mersey. [DP034209]*

CHAPTER 2

In the beginning

Liverpool in the Middle Ages was little more than a fishing village and did not even rate parish status, being part of the distant parish of St Mary, Walton. A chapel close to the quay was built *c*1360, dedicated to Our Lady and St Nicholas (Fig 2), Christendom's universal protectress and a saint renowned for calming a storm. A smaller chapel, St Mary-del-Quay, stood in the churchyard, and nearby, it is said, was a statue of St Nicholas to which departing seafarers addressed their prayers. For centuries, this was the only provision for worship which the small settlement required.

The immediate impact on Liverpool of the religious Reformation of Henry VIII's reign (1509–47) was consequently relatively slight, for Liverpool boasted no shrines and monastic churches for the king's commissioners to despoil and close. Many accepted the momentous

Figure 2 (right) *The earliest surviving view of the medieval Church of Our Lady and St Nicholas, built c1360 and altered by the addition of a spire in 1746. [Engraving by E Rooker after P P Burdett (1773)]*

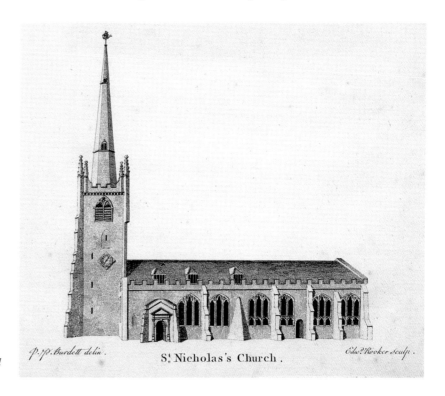

P. W. Burdett delin. S.ᵗ Nicholas's Church. *Edwᵈ Rooker sculp.*

(left) *Liverpool's original parish church, St Mary's Church, Walton, as it looked in 1839. [Liverpool Record Office, Liverpool Libraries, Small Prints Collection]*

religious changes decreed by king and Parliament; Evan Nicholas, last Catholic priest of Our Lady and St Nicholas's became its first Protestant minister. Despite the efforts of preachers sent to instruct the people in the reformed religion, many remained loyal to the traditions of the pre-Reformation Catholic church. Only when Queen Elizabeth I (1558–1603) established the Church of England on a firm footing were the lingering hopes of a reconciliation with Rome extinguished, and many young Lancashire gentlemen left home for the Catholic seminaries of Europe, later to return as missionary priests. Catholicism became a secret and illegal devotion, sustained on the estates of recusant gentry, including many of the families in the Liverpool area – the Molyneux family of Croxteth Hall, the Blundells of Ince Blundell, the Norris family of Speke and the Fazakerleys of Fazakerley. Despite the high price to be paid for loyalty to the old religion, by the beginning of the 17th century rural Lancashire had the largest Catholic community in England.

In contrast to the loyalties of the countryside, Lancashire towns such as Liverpool and Manchester became centres of Puritan sentiment. In 1612, for example, Thomas Wainwright – the clerk of Our Lady and St Nicholas's, apparently susceptible to the foppish fashions of the Stuart Court – was instructed by the Corporation to wear the sober surplice of his office and to cut his hair to 'a comly and seemly length in such decent manner as best befitteth a man in his place'.[1] Some time between 1604 and 1618, the first dissenting chapel, for a Presbyterian congregation, was built in Toxteth, then a relatively remote rural park on the outskirts of the town (Fig 3).

By the end of the 17th century Liverpool was a growing town inadequately provided with churches. It was governed by an increasingly prosperous Protestant mercantile elite suspicious of the Catholic sympathies of many of their socially superior landed neighbours and conscious of the proximity of Ireland, that land of political unrest and a Catholic majority.

Figure 3 *The Ancient Chapel of Toxteth, where notorious Puritan Richard Mather preached from 1618 until his enforced emigration to New England in 1635. The chapel was substantially rebuilt in 1774. In common with many early Presbyterian chapels, it is now Unitarian. [AA040988]*

CHAPTER 3

God versus Mammon

The arrival in 1648 of the first cargo of goods from America was to herald the transformation of the town's fortunes: Liverpool was poised to emerge as one of the world's richest cities. But compared to its rivals, London and Bristol, Liverpool lacked an impressive skyline of ecclesiastical towers and spires, while its citizens had to be buried in far away Walton or the overcrowded churchyard attached to the medieval chapel of Our Lady and St Nicholas. Citizens of the expanding town felt these deficiencies keenly. By the end of the 17th century the population had risen to about 6,000 and Our Lady and St Nicholas's could not seat even half of those who wanted to attend church.

In 1699 the Corporation decided that the town's growing prominence should be recognised by the creation of a separate parish. The parish church of Walton was too far away, on a route lined with distractions causing young men to fall into sin on the Sabbath. Furthermore, the patron of St Mary's Church in Walton was the Catholic recusant Lord Molyneux. The Act of Parliament by which the parish of Liverpool was created reflects the town's sense of its own importance: Liverpool is described as 'now the third port of the trade of England and pays upwards of £50,000 per annum to the King … . Many new streets are built and are still in building; and many gentlemen's sons … are put apprentices of the town.'[2]

The act was passed and the new Church of St Peter, still close to open fields, was consecrated in 1704 (Fig 4). St Peter's was only a beginning, for the Corporation went on to support an 18th-century church building boom consolidating Liverpool's claim to be one of the principal towns of the realm. A further four new churches were built, each one requiring an Act of Parliament. St George's (Thomas Steers, 1726–34), provided with a spire at the express instructions of the Corporation, was adopted as the principal civic church, and members of the town's leading families were buried in its crypt. Liverpool's Corporation churches were all provided with eye-catching towers and spires as the 18th-century builders intended to provide the town with a skyline resembling that of a much older town – Timothy Lightholer's neo-Classical Church of St Paul (1763–9), for example, shared both a domed silhouette and a dedication with Sir Christopher Wren's more

(left) *The medieval Church of Our Lady and St Nicholas dwarfed by Liverpool's bustling Victorian port.* [The Port of Liverpool, 1873, *by Samuel Walters, National Museums Liverpool, Walker Art Gallery]*

Figure 4 (above) *St Peter's was the first new church to be built after the creation of the parish of Liverpool. It opened in 1704 and in 1880 it became the pro-cathedral of the newly-created diocese of Liverpool. It was demolished in 1922 when the first parts of the new cathedral in Upper Duke Street were consecrated. This photograph was taken in 1903. [BB45/1518]*

Figure 5 *The striking Paradise Street Unitarian Chapel of 1791 was founded by the expanding congregation of the old Presbyterian Chapel in Key Street. In 1849 the congregation abandoned the chapel in favour of a new building in the more salubrious Hope Street. [Redrawn after 19th-century engravings]*

famous London cathedral. In 1746 a spire was even added to Our Lady and St Nicholas's.

The Corporation was not the only church builder. Unlike the Church of England, the Nonconformist denominations were not held back by the need for an Act of Parliament, and a small number of Liverpool's dissenting chapels warranted inclusion in the earliest guides to the town. Liverpool's Unitarians, always relatively small in number, were disproportionately influential in the religious, cultural and political life of the town. William Roscoe, poet, historian and man of letters, elected to represent Liverpool in Parliament in 1806, was a member of the Benn's Garden congregation, for example, as was bookseller and publisher John Gore, who published the town's first directory in 1776. The octagonal Unitarian Chapel in Paradise Street (1791) was of particular architectural distinction (Fig 5).

While the buildings of the Established Church and the Nonconformists were prominent and eye-catching, and their clergymen were among the town's most prominent citizens, Catholic worship in Liverpool remained clandestine and largely hidden from view. Following the Jacobite Rebellion of 1745, the modest chapel in Lumber Street was destroyed in 1746 by a Protestant mob, only to be rebuilt, disguised as a warehouse. In the 19th century the chapel was rebuilt once again as St Mary's, Highfield Street. Despite the violent Gordon Riots that followed

Figure 6 *St Peter's Catholic Chapel was built in 1788 before the Second Catholic Relief Act of 1791 legalised public Catholic worship. The memory of recent riotous attacks on Catholic buildings no doubt influenced its low-key character. The chapel was enlarged in 1817 and 1845. It is now a fashionable restaurant.* [DP034208]

the passing of the First Catholic Relief Act of 1778, life gradually became easier for Catholics in the course of the 18th century. The Second Catholic Relief Act of 1791 finally allowed them to worship in public and to build churches for the first time since the Reformation, although their chapels could have neither bells nor steeples. Of Liverpool's three 18th-century Catholic chapels, only one – St Peter's, in Seel Street (Fig 6), built in 1788 – has survived, although it is now in secular use. In common with many Catholic chapels built in the penal years, it has a modest and unassuming exterior, barely distinguishable from a Nonconformist chapel. Its galleried interior has survived conversion into commercial premises.

Another place of worship in Seel Street that could easily have been mistaken for a Nonconformist chapel was Liverpool's first purpose-built synagogue, designed in 1807 by John Harrison of Chester. The first synagogue and burial ground had been established by 1753 in Synagogue Court, off Stanley Street, a rather insalubrious part of town. In December 1778 the Corporation assigned to Jewish trustees a house in Frederick Street, a far better neighbourhood, that accommodated 50 to 70 worshippers, which the congregation soon outgrew. The new Seel Street Synagogue, on the corner of Colquitt Street, was a handsome building with a façade of Ionic columns. It accommodated 290 worshippers and cost the substantial sum of over £2,000, subscribed by 35 families. The origins of these earliest Jewish 'Liverpolitans' are suggested by the language of the congregation's earliest book of rules, which is in a mixture of Hebrew, Polish, German and Yiddish. Liverpool's 18th-century Jews were pedlars and itinerant merchants, but prospered and assimilated quickly, anglicising their names. The 1790 Liverpool Directory lists 20 Jewish households, and in 1797 4 Jews were among the founders of the Athenaeum and its attached library.

With the exception of St Peter's, Seel Street, none of Liverpool's 18th-century city-centre places of worship has survived, having been subsequently sacrificed to a combination of commercial redevelopment and declining population in the city centre. Precious land closest to the expanding port was devoted to the pursuit of the wealth and mercantile success that was to make the port of Liverpool second in importance only to London.

CHAPTER 4

Worshipping with the wealthy

While the Corporation took the lead in establishing new churches, their endeavours did not keep pace with the spread of the town. The population increased from around 26,000 in the 1760s, to almost 80,000 by 1801 and a staggering 376,000 by 1851. As Liverpool spread ever further from its historic dockside core, its more prosperous citizens moved out of the commercial districts, separating their homes from their warehouses and places of business in search of picturesque and semi-rural seclusion. Enterprising individuals developed new residential districts, and no stylish new neighbourhood could hope to thrive without a commodious church or chapel at its heart. The building of new churches and chapels took on the character of a private enterprise.

Speculative enterprise

The Church of St Anne in St Anne's Street was erected 1770–2 in one of Liverpool's best neighbourhoods to the north of the town centre at the expense of a Mr Dobb and fellow subscribers. On the southern edge of the town the Church of St James, St James Place, Toxteth, was erected and perhaps designed by builder and cabinet maker Cuthbert Bisbrown (Fig 7). It was to be the showpiece of a speculative residential

Figure 7 (right) *No longer in use for worship and now in the care of the Churches Conservation Trust, the plain brick exterior of St James's belies its historical importance in the history of cast-iron engineering. [DP034182]*

(left) *The choir of Ullet Road Unitarian Church, with windows by Morris & Co. [AA040397]*

development, a new town to be called 'Harrington' in honour of the family of the Countess of Sefton, whose husband owned Toxteth Park, still an undeveloped rural area on the fringe of the growing town. Bisbrown had borrowed heavily, but his enterprise was not blessed with financial success: after attracting the investment of 27 subscribers and in 1774 building the church at a cost of £3,000 (and building a few houses nearby), he was declared bankrupt.

Both St Anne's and St James's were constructed of brick with stone dressings and externally neither was architecturally exceptional. They are remarkable milestones in the history of engineering, however, as both buildings used structural cast iron in the columns to support their galleries. In the early 18th century cast iron had been used for decorative embellishment. Its use for structural support was to transform industrial architecture, making it light and fireproof, but one of its earliest surviving structural uses in the country is in the Church of St James in Liverpool (Fig 8), for St Anne's was destroyed during the Second World War.

Figure 8 *A remarkable survival: the cast-iron columns that support the gallery of St James's Church. [DP034183]*

Clerical celebrity

The success of several Liverpool churches and chapels reflected the celebrity of a successful minister. St Bride's (1829–30, Fig 9) is a Classically chaste temple with Ionic portico situated on the east side of the newly developed Percy Street; it was built at the expense of private subscribers for the Revd James Haldane Stewart (d1854), the popular minister of a failed London proprietary chapel. Great George Street Congregational Chapel was built in 1811 for the charismatic and youthful preacher Revd Thomas Spencer of the Newington Chapel in Renshaw Street. This original Great George Street Congregational Chapel was destroyed by fire in 1840, but such was its popularity, attracting congregations of unprecedented size thanks to the oratorical skills of Spencer and his successor Revd Thomas Raffles, that the money needed for a new building was collected within a few weeks. Its successor (Fig 10), which opened in October 1841, takes full advantage of its prominent site at the junction of Great George Street and Nelson Street, on a major

Figure 9 *Samuel Rowland's St Bride's, Percy Street (1829–30), is the perfect Greek temple in the service of the Church of England. It is the only intact ecclesiastical survivor in the Classical style once so popular with Liverpool church and chapel builders.* [AA040567]

Figure 10 *The outstanding building of Liverpool Congregationalism, Great George Street Congregational Chapel, was designed by Corporation surveyor Joseph Franklin and opened in 1841. It is affectionately know as 'The Blackie' because of its once sooty exterior.* [AA040498]

thoroughfare south of Toxteth Park. Now in secular use, the chapel has lost its once dramatic galleried interior and only the vestibule inside the semicircular portico of fluted Corinthian columns remains unaltered.

Cast-iron Gothic

During the 18th and early 19th century Liverpool was a town in love with the architectural styles of the Classical past. Only two of its Corporation churches, St John's (1763–9) and St Luke's, St Luke's Place (foundation stone laid in 1811), had been built in a Gothic style. While St Luke's survives as a conspicuous and impressive example of the early Gothic Revival, St John's was soon to be overshadowed and outshone by the glory of its neighbour, Harvey Lonsdale Elmes's Classical St George's Hall, begun in 1841. The strong hold of neo-Classicism over Liverpool's church and chapel builders is no longer readily apparent because many of their buildings have been destroyed or demolished, leaving St Bride's, Percy Street, and Great George Street Congregational Chapel as two of the few survivors of Classicism's supremacy in Liverpool.

The most popular alternative to Classical architecture in church building was Gothic, and Liverpool played an important part in the revival of interest in medieval styles. One of the most energetic and idiosyncratic private patrons of Anglican church building was Liverpool iron-founder John Cragg of the Mersey Iron Foundry. Having made his money manufacturing pans used for boiling sugar from the West Indies, Cragg channelled his energies into promoting the structural use of iron. In 1809, intending to build in semi-rural Toxteth Park, he had employed architect Joseph Gandy to assist in the design of a church. In the same year he registered his first patent for a new building technique involving cast-iron structural roof elements combined with panels of slate.

Cragg's obsession with cast-iron construction was matched by his enthusiasm for the Gothic style. When Gandy left Liverpool in 1812 Cragg took on the sometime medical practitioner, Quaker and antiquary Thomas Rickman. Rickman's 'apprenticeship' with Cragg was never an easy one, but provided him with the springboard for a successful career

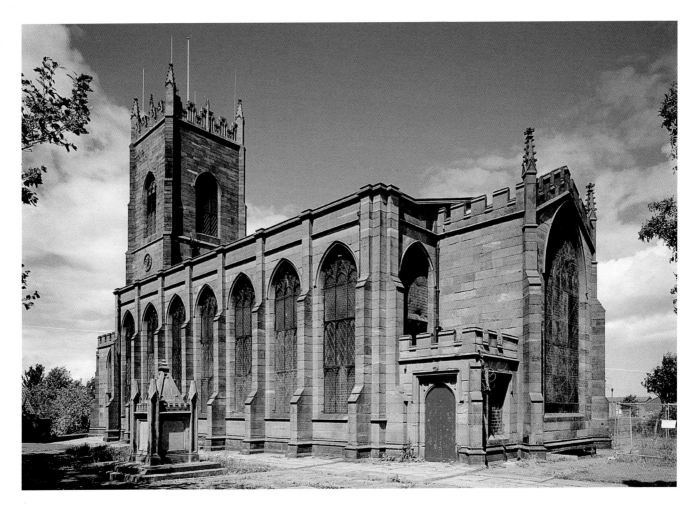

Figure 11 *The sober stone exterior of St George's, Everton (1813–14), does little to prepare the visitor for the spectacular lightness and delicacy of the interior.* *[AA040980]*

in the architectural profession. While working for Cragg he composed his landmark book, *An Attempt to Discriminate the Styles of English Architecture from the Conquest to the Reformation*, published in 1817, in which he established a vocabulary of architectural style used to describe Gothic to this day.

In 1813 Cragg seized the chance to put his constructional ideas and Rickman's Gothic designs into practice, becoming a subscriber to and the builder of St George's, Heyworth Street, in Everton (Fig 11). The church was designed in the Perpendicular Gothic style and has a conventional external appearance, built of stone and employing iron only for window tracery and buttress pinnacles (since removed). Inside, despite the

Figure 12 (left) *John Cragg intended this cast-iron traceried tour de force, St George's, Everton, to serve as a showcase for both his foundry's products and the Gothic style. [AA040984]*

removal of the original western gallery later in the 19th century, the interior still impresses (Fig 12), with its delicate cast-iron columns and its delightfully traceried ceiling.

Some of the elements of St George's, especially the tracery of the east window, reappear in the construction of Cragg's second church, St Michael in the Hamlet (1813–15). However, the constructional techniques employed in this church were in a more developed form, reflecting a new patent registered in 1813. The church resembles a medieval Cheshire country church (Fig 13), well suited to the picturesque village setting Cragg sought in the development of his new suburban hamlet by the river. It stood in the midst of an artful cluster of picturesque villas, one occupied by Cragg himself, also constructed with

Figure 13 (below) *In the construction of the Church of St Michael in the Hamlet Cragg made bolder use of prefabricated cast-iron elements, identifiable by their protective red paint. [AA040977]*

cast-iron elements. Closer inspection of the church reveals the novelty of its construction, with thin slate panels, originally sanded to take on the appearance of stone, encasing its brick shell at dado and clerestory levels. As with St George's, cast iron is also used for windows, tracery, parapet and pinnacles, and the interior is characterised by the decorative use of slender iron columns and delicate tracery.

If Cragg was an evangelist of the Gothic style, he was also a hard-headed Liverpool businessman eager to promote the technical and financial advantages of his own products. His 1809 patent had already explained the benefits of prefabricated iron parts, which could be manufactured in Liverpool and exported through her port for erection in the colonies. The parts could be transported easily and cheaply as ballast in the holds of Liverpool's trading fleet. In the 1813 patent, illustrated with drawings of St Michael's in the Hamlet, Cragg described how his system could achieve an affordable version of Gothic: his materials were light and durable and the delicate (and thus costly) intricacies of Gothic carving could easily be replicated in the casting process. The practical vindication of Cragg's prefabricated system came in 1900 when the north wall of St Michael's in the Hamlet was easily dismantled to admit an aisle extension. His third iron church, St Philip's, Hardman Street (1816), was closed in 1882.

High church, low church

While John Cragg's great wealth was employed to promote the Gothic style and the products of his foundry, the wealth of the Horsfall family was used to promote its members' personal taste in churchmanship. Three generations of the family had a major impact on church building in Liverpool. C H Horsfall, a successful merchant and stockbroker, had been one of the founders of St George's, Everton, and his sons built Christ Church, Great Homer Street (E H Shellard, 1848), in his memory. His son, Robert, and grandson, Douglas, became strong advocates of the ritualism of the Oxford Movement, which in the 1840s and 1850s led a revival of interest in the traditions of the pre-Reformation English church. Ritualists sought to reconnect England with the liturgical practices of the medieval past, placing Holy Communion once more at the heart of worship. This theological revival was matched by a growing interest in the architecture and furnishings of the medieval church. To their opponents, supporters of the Oxford Movement were little better than closet Roman Catholics, a suspicion confirmed by a number of defections to Rome by high-profile Anglicans of whom John Henry Newman, later Cardinal Newman, was the most famous.

Robert Horsfall built St Margaret's of Antioch in Princes Road (1868–9) as a place of high church worship, a tradition to which the church adheres to this day. It was designed by the London architect George Edmund Street and helped to establish his national reputation. The church and its vicarage are set back from the road and the vicarage is positioned at an angle to both the church and the street, creating a natural, almost semi-rural feel to the setting. Now gradually being restored to glory, the church interior is one of the richest in Liverpool (Fig 14). The interior is designed to appeal to the senses, with every surface coloured and decorated, and the chancel is raised above the level of the five-bay nave, underlining the importance of the celebration of the Eucharist. As with his architect, Horsfall employed national as well as local firms of church decorators, including Clayton & Bell of London (wall-paintings and stained glass) and Skidmore of Coventry (metalwork). Careful neither to praise nor to condemn the churchmanship of the first vicar, the controversial ritualist Revd Charles Parnell, Liverpool's historian J A Picton, himself an architect, acknowledged that 'architectural truth and earnestness are visible in every line'.[3] Parnell turned St Margaret's into the headquarters of ritualism in Liverpool, but attempts to persuade the Bishop of Chester to use the 1840 Church Discipline Act to censure him came to nothing. Full-scale war was averted when in 1879 Parnell relinquished his post. His successor, the former curate James Bell Cox, was less fortunate. Bishop Ryle, first bishop of the newly created Anglican diocese of Liverpool, himself a low-church evangelical, was persuaded, somewhat reluctantly, to prosecute Cox for irregular practices, and he was briefly imprisoned.

Figure 14 *'The beauty of holiness' beloved of the adherents of the Oxford Movement, expressed in the extraordinarily rich decor of G E Street's St Margaret's of Antioch, Princes Road. Despite being at the epicentre of the notorious Toxteth riots of 1981, and in an area of serious social deprivation, St Margaret's remains cherished by its neighbourhood and remains unscathed by serious vandalism. [DP034184]*

The controversy was fuelled by the building of St Agnes's, Ullet Road (1883–5), on the edge of affluent Sefton Park (Fig 15). It was the creation of Douglas Horsfall, also a ritualist, who like his father, also favoured architects with a national reputation. For St Agnes's he employed John Loughborough Pearson, architect of Truro Cathedral. St Agnes's is one of Pearson's finest churches, an essay in 13th-century elegance. Its nave, with circular piers with moulded capitals and strongly accented triforium, is in an English idiom, while its apsidal east end and slender lancets are reminiscent of a High Gothic French church (Fig 16).

Figure 15 *The brick exterior of J L Pearson's St Agnes's, Ullet Road, in fashionable Sefton Park, built in 1883–5 for stockbroker Douglas Horsfall at a cost of £28,000. [AA041051]*

Figure 16 *The stone-faced vaulted interior of St Agnes's, described by Nikolaus Pevsner as 'the most beautiful Victorian church in Liverpool'. [AA045366]*

The exterior is of brick with stone dressings, but the interior is ashlar-faced and stone-vaulted, accentuating the cathedral-like sense of great space and height. This most perfect of Gothic churches was designed to be the backdrop to services that recalled the Catholic past of pre-Reformation England. Even before it opened the churchmanship of Horsfall and his chosen clergyman, Revd Charles Elam, attracted controversy. Bishop Ryle required Elam to sign an undertaking not to use altar lights or sing the *Agnus Dei* in the Roman Catholic fashion. During consecration of the church Protestant Orangemen protested outside.

Princes Park

By 1860 very few of Liverpool's wealthier citizens still lived in the town centre. In the second half of the 19th century desirable new housing was springing up on the edges of the contrived landscapes of Liverpool's newly established public parks. The earliest was Princes Park, laid out from 1842 by Joseph Paxton and James Pennethorne. The residents of Princes Park were exceptionally well served by places of worship, and one of the most striking characteristics of the neighbourhood is the extraordinary diversity of faiths and denominations represented in such a small geographic area. The Roman Catholics are the only group conspicuous by their absence. On Belvidere Road the 1846–8 'parish' church of St Paul by A H Holme (demolished) was in close proximity to the 1856 Presbyterian Church (converted to residential use), also on Belvidere Road, and the 1861–2 St John's Wesleyan Methodist Church (now the Belvidere Road Independent Baptist Church).

The principal thoroughfare from the town was Princes Road, laid out in 1843, to which the parallel Princes Avenue was added in 1870. This created a wide boulevard with a tree-lined central reservation that accommodated the tram lines that conveyed the residents to and from the congested bustle of the old town; these lines remained until the early 1960s though the last Liverpool tram ran in 1956. These roads were lined with an extraordinary display of ecclesiastical buildings. The most spectacular group of survivors comprises the former Welsh Presbyterian Church (W & G Audsley, 1865–8), the Greek Orthodox Church of St Nicholas (Henry Sumners, 1870), the Church of England's St Margaret's of Antioch (G E Street, 1868–9) and the Old Hebrew Congregation Synagogue (W & G Audsley, 1871–4, Fig 17). The Ibo Centre, formerly the Adult Deaf and Dumb Institute (E H Banner, 1886–7), although not a church, was a charitable institution founded on Church of England principles, and a striking octagonal chapel with

Figure 17 *The removal of the small domes from the octagonal turrets of its main façade has done little to diminish the eastern exoticism of the Old Hebrew Congregation Synagogue in Princes Road.* [AA040894]

raked seating occupies its upper storey. These buildings were all designed for public display and represented a high-water mark in the confidence and prosperity of their congregations. The Welsh Presbyterian Church, home of Liverpool's single largest congregation of Welsh Calvinist Methodism, is especially interesting in this respect. By 1870 there was said to be over 20,000 Welsh-born residents of Liverpool, a figure that had risen to 80,000 by 1891. Their wealth had been founded on property and it is said that Sunday mornings outside the chapel were characterised by the rustle of silk, as the wives of wealthy Welsh businessmen promenaded nearby. Their new chapel was built in an eye-catching French Gothic style to an ambitious T-shaped plan, with an impressive north-west spire. It has been closed for many years and has been a building at risk for some time, with its interior stripped and its roof only recently stabilised after its partial collapse.

By 1874 Liverpool's prosperous orthodox Jewish residents found Seel Street inconveniently far from their homes, while the character of the area had changed for the worse. A competition for a design for a building in fashionable Princes Road was won by W & G Audsley, whose work would have been familiar to them from the nearby Welsh Presbyterian Church. For the synagogue the Audsleys sought a very different architectural style. A growing interest in the archaeology and architecture of the Middle East, and especially in the sites of Jerusalem, was formative in meeting their brief, and the Audsleys preferred eastern exoticism over more conventional Gothic Revivalism. They described their design as being 'with enough of the eastern style to render it suggestive and enough western severity to make it appropriate for a street building in an English town'.[4] When it opened on 3 September 1874 it attracted enthusiastic press interest in Liverpool and beyond.

It cost nearly £15,000, and its interior is one of the most remarkable in the city, being of the finest quality and craftsmanship (Fig 18). Its success established the national reputation of the Audleys as synagogue architects and they went on to design the New West End Synagogue in London's Bayswater (1877–9), a smaller version of the Liverpool building. These two buildings are among the finest of England's surviving 'cathedral synagogues' and Princes Road has recently been described as

Figure 18 (left) *With its sumptuous marble bimar in the foreground and its richly decorated ark at the east end, the Old Hebrew Congregation Synagogue is one of the most spectacular of Liverpool's 19th-century interiors and England's most lavish High Victorian synagogue. [AA028040]*

Figure 19 *The Greek Orthodox Church of St Nicholas was influenced by a growing interest in the architecture of the Middle East, being a smaller-scale version of the Church of St Theodore in Constantinople (modern-day Istanbul). [AA040893]*

the 'most lavish High Victorian 'orientalist' synagogue in England, a jewel in the crown of Europe's "Capital of Culture" 2008'.[5] Princes Road has recently been relisted at Grade I in recognition of its exceptional quality, making it one of only three Grade I-listed synagogues in the country.

Another exotic building is the Greek Orthodox Church of St Nicholas on Berkeley Street, visible from Princes Road, which opened in 1870 (Fig 19). The Greek community was small but prosperous, deriving its wealth from shipping, and had formerly worshipped in a private house. In 1864 a competition to design a new church was won by W & J Hay, although the design was eventually to be executed by Henry Sumners, for reasons that remain obscure. The multiple domes of the exterior make it one of the most eye-catching buildings in the city, although contemporary commentators were ambivalent about its architectural merits.

Sefton Park

Liverpool's largest public park opened in 1872. As with Princes Park, it was intended that the sale of residential plots in Sefton Park would defray the costs of the landscaping. Horsfall's St Agnes's was far from the only church to serve its residents, for Sefton Park was another neighbourhood of outstanding ecclesiastical buildings. By the 1880s Liverpool's Catholics were achieving wealth and social acceptance reflected in the Church of St Clare, Arundel Avenue (1889–90) by Leonard Stokes, paid for by Francis and James Reynolds, wealthy cotton brokers (Fig 20). It is one of the most original and dramatic churches of the period, although the budget for the building was limited (it cost only £7,834), meaning that its upper walls are of painted plaster rather than the stone that Stokes intended. Its furnishings are nonetheless of exceptional quality (Fig 21).

Figure 20 *The imaginative use of pierced internal wall buttresses to create circulatory aisles reveals the influence of the medieval cathedral of Albi in south-west France and makes St Clare's one of the most innovative of Liverpool 19th-century church designs. [AA045357]*

Figure 21 (right) *The high east wall of St Clare's, accommodates the sumptuous 1890 reredos by Robert Anning Bell and George Frampton, relieving the austerity of this lofty interior. [AA045359]*

Figure 22 *Ullet Road Unitarian Church was the third building constructed by Liverpool's wealthy and influential Unitarians and unquestionably the finest. It was designed in 1896 by Thomas and Percy Worthington of Manchester, themselves Unitarians.* [AA040437]

Figure 23 *The timbered hall of Ullet Road Unitarian Church, the gift of Sir John Brunner and sugar-magnate Henry Tate, connected to the church by a medieval-style cloister. [AA040410]*

After St Agnes's and St Clare's, the third surviving jewel in the Sefton Park crown is the Ullet Road Unitarian Church (Fig 22). English Unitarianism grew out of a variety of strands of Puritan dissent, all characterised by a rational interpretation of the Scriptures and a liberal approach to personal belief. As many Unitarians did not subscribe to a belief in the Trinity, the denomination remained illegal until 1813. Liverpool's Unitarians formed a small but distinguished community of liberal and successful businessmen, merchants and entrepreneurs, some of the wealthiest and most prominent families in Liverpool, including the Holts, the Tates, the Roscoes, the Rathbones and the Brunners. The congregation had moved from Renshaw Street (on the site of Methodist Central Hall, now itself converted for commercial use), preserving monuments from the earliest church, which are now displayed in the cloister that links the church and hall in an attractive collegiate complex. The church and library were built in 1896–9, with the hall (Fig 23) and the linking cloister added in 1901–2. It is one of the most outstanding repositories of Arts and Crafts craftsmanship anywhere in the country (Fig 24).

The rapid expansion of Liverpool had outstripped the ability of either Established Church or Corporation to keep pace with the demand for new places of worship in popular new suburbs. Liverpool's wealthy applied the entrepreneurial skills honed in business to the planting of new churches, chapels and synagogues for their families and their servants. Their tastes, whether architectural or in terms of churchmanship, determined the nature of some of Liverpool's finest 18th- and 19th-century buildings. The poor worshippers of Liverpool, in contrast, exerted an influence on church building not through an expression of their tastes but through their sheer weight of numbers.

Figure 24 *Every Arts and Crafts detail at Ullet Road Unitarian Church, down to the metalwork on windows and doors, is of exceptional quality. [AA040409]*

CHAPTER 5

Blessed are the poor

By the middle of the 19th century Liverpool had one of the highest population densities and one of the lowest rates of life expectancy of any city in the country. In the 1840s the work of Dr William Henry Duncan, underlined by the typhus outbreak of 1847 and the cholera outbreak of 1849, had established the link between poverty, poor housing, inadequate sanitation and death from disease.

Churchgoing c1850

While the Liverpool Sanitary Act of 1846 began the long battle for a cleaner and healthier town, Liverpool's spiritual health was perceived as a problem more intractable. Liverpool had too few churches for its growing population and the fastest growing poorer neighbourhoods were especially badly served. While the overall population of Liverpool only increased by 5 per cent in the period 1851–61, Toxteth had experienced 11 per cent growth, Kirkdale 63 per cent, Everton 112 per cent and Edge Hill a massive 198 per cent. Furthermore, in many churches the better-off paid an annual rent for the exclusive use of a pew, excluding the poor and limiting the amount of space for 'free' seats. It was widely recognised that church accommodation for the poor was inadequate, and even where free pews were provided, the lack of a suit of 'Sunday best' deterred many poorer people from attending church regularly (Fig 25). The challenge of getting the working-class poor into church and away from the perils of alcohol and vice preoccupied the clergy of all denominations.

Revd Abraham Hume (1814–84), vicar of All Souls' Church in Vauxhall, a trained mathematician, used statistical analysis to understand the root of the problem and published his own evaluation of the 1851 census figures. He estimated that in 1851, the year in which four new Liverpool parishes were created, the Church of England could still accommodate only 15 per cent of worshippers. By 1858 it was estimated that 40 out of every 100 Liverpool citizens did not attend church on Sunday. Hume's research also highlighted the fact that churches were not in the right place to serve the most pressing need. People would not travel far to attend church, so larger churches did not necessarily lead to larger

Pressed concrete relief, the children's cloister, St Christopher's, Norris Green. [DP034194]

Figure 25 *The residents of No 2 Court, Silvester Street, many of the children barefoot, pose for the photographer in July 1913. [Liverpool Record Office, Liverpool Libraries 352 HOU 82/19]*

congregations; churches within a few streets of home were what was needed. In the 1850s and 1860s the area north of Tithebarn Street and the town centre exemplified the problems that Hume had identified. The population of the district had grown quickly as the docks spread northwards. By *c*1860 the area had a population of nearly 27,000, packed into street upon street of insanitary and overcrowded cellar and courtyard dwellings. They were served by only two Anglican churches: St Martin's in the Fields, constructed in 1828 with a grant from the Church Commissioners, and St Augustine's, Shaw Street, of 1830. In contrast, the Church of St Philip, Hardman Street, served a well-to-do district of only 590 residents. Hume advocated the reorganisation of district boundaries to achieve more equitable distribution of population among the churches. The shortcomings of the clergy could only be addressed by the better endowment of their churches and by breaking the reliance on pew rents.

Poor levels of church attendance were also of concern in Catholic circles. In 1843 it was estimated that as many as 40,000 Catholics could find no place in church and in 1855 it was reckoned that only 37.5 per cent of resident Catholics attended Easter Mass. In 1850 the Roman Catholic episcopal hierarchy was restored in England, and Liverpool, with its large Catholic population, was an obvious choice for a new bishopric. Under Bishop Brown's leadership, the increasingly self-confident clergy mobilised the resources needed to implement an ambitious programme of church and school construction. Indeed, a school would often precede the church. The achievement was an astonishing one, given the poverty of the community that supported it with their donations. Bishop Brown realised that the fund-raising initiatives of the wealthier Catholic laity had led to proprietary arrangements similar to those found in many Anglican churches. Henceforth, the control of church building was in the hands of the clergy, and battle was joined in the war to entice the poor back into the fold.

Building for the poor

Very few buildings survive to give an impression of the church-going experience in Liverpool's poor neighbourhoods in the middle of the 19th century. Most were built in some variation of the Gothic style, but many were modest in scale and simple in form (Fig 26). Many working-class

Figure 26 *The simple Church of St Clement, Beaumont Street (George Williams & Arthur Yates), was built in 1841 in an area once semi-rural but fast becoming heavily populated, working class and poor. [AA036003]*

Liverpool Anglicans remained resolutely low church, preferring services in which the sermon remained far more important than Holy Communion. Their churches were generally unaisled boxes, with galleries on three sides, and with only a shallow recess for the altar. Indeed, the altar was often obscured by the centrally placed towering pulpit and clerk's desk, the most dramatic piece of furnishing in the building, allowing the preacher to rain down words of fire on his congregation (Fig 27). The parishioners would be seated in box pews with doors, each pew numbered to identify its rent-paying occupants (Fig 28). The free seats, usually with a poor view of the pulpit, were situated at the back of the church or in the gallery.

Figure 27 *The view from the pulpit. The interior of St Clement's is a well-preserved example of a low-church preaching box once common in Liverpool. On census Sunday in 1851 over 300 people worshipped here. [AA036006]*

Figure 28 *A sample of church seating in Liverpool.*

The arrangement and styles of church seating can often reveal a great deal about patterns of worship.

The plans below show the arrangement of pews at the foot of the towering pulpit at St Clement's Church, Beaumont Street, a fiercely evangelical preaching church built in 1843. By 2005 the pulpit had been remodelled and rows of pews removed, reflecting smaller congregations, but also freeing up space for social and community activities.

Original features are often lost when seating is modernised. The numbered pews with their umbrella fittings preserved at Christ Church, Linnet Lane (1870–1), are evidence of the social habits of an earlier generation of churchgoers and were once common in Liverpool's Protestant and Catholic churches and chapels alike (right). *The doors protected the pew's occupants from uncomfortable draughts. By this date numbered pews with doors were relatively rare, having been widely attacked for their social exclusivity.*

Extra seating for festivals and High Mass was provided at the Catholic Church of Our Lady of Reconciliation de la Salette in Eldon Street (1859–60) by the ingenious use of fold-down extensions (below right). *The kneeling boards could also be folded up when not in use.*

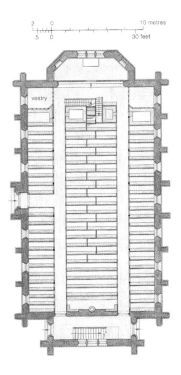

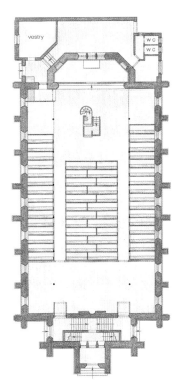

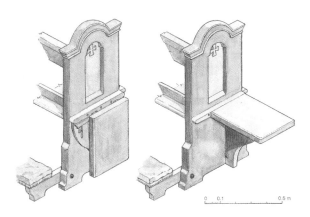

The enormous increase in the numbers of Catholic residents of the North End in the 1830s and 1840s triggered a furious spate of church building. The Church of St Anthony of Egypt, Scotland Road (Fig 29), was constructed in 1833 on the site of the former 'French Chapel'. Father Jean Baptiste Geradot had arrived in Liverpool in 1793, a refugee from the French Revolution, and in 1804 built the first Catholic chapel in Liverpool to be served by secular priests. The new church was designed by Rickman's pupil John Broadbent and yet the Gothic of St Anthony's is barely skin deep, for behind its ashlar Gothic façade the church is an aisleless stuccoed brick box with lancet windows and a flat coffered

Figure 29 *Behind its Gothic façade only the richness of its sanctuary distinguishes the Church of St Anthony of Egypt, Scotland Road, from a late Georgian Nonconformist preaching box. [AA041009]*

Figure 30 *During the Second World War the crypt of St Anthony's, built as the last resting place of the faithful departed, offered shelter to the living, driven underground by the bombing of the North End.* [AA041004]

ceiling. This is the kind of building on which the Catholic architect and champion of the Gothic Revival A W N Pugin (1812–52) would have poured scorn. The most Gothic aspect of St Anthony's is also the least visible: the atmospheric groin-vaulted brick crypt that runs the length of the building (Figs 30 and 31).

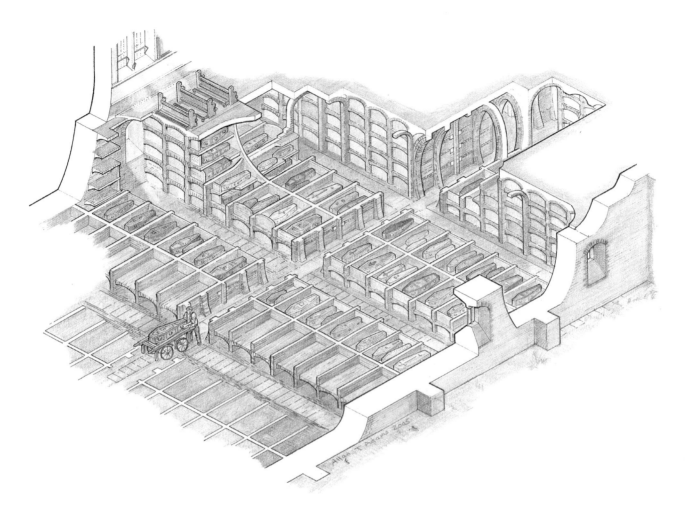

The close proximity of St Anthony's; St Alban's, Athol Street (1849, now a climbing centre, *see* Fig 64); Our Lady of Reconciliation de la Salette, Eldon Street, Vauxhall (1859–60); All Souls', Collingwood Street (1870, demolished); St Bridget's, Bevington Hill (1870, rebuilt 1894, demolished) and St Sylvester's, Silvester Street (1889), emphasises the density of the Catholic population of the North End as a consequence of Irish immigration, especially in the years after the potato famine. There was an urgent need for maximum church accommodation at minimum cost, a demand admirably met in the churches designed by Pugin's eldest son, Edward Welby Pugin. Pugin honed a design that was spacious,

Figure 31 *The crypt of St Anthony's runs the full length of the church and is Catholic Liverpool's oldest surviving place of burial and the focus of a new community heritage initiative.*

Figure 32 *Our Lady of Reconciliation de la Salette, Eldon Street, was once hemmed in on every side by narrow streets of tightly packed terraced houses. Little light could be expected to penetrate at street level, so its high clerestory windows were of paramount importance. [AA040970]*

Figure 33 *Inside the Church of Our Lady of Reconciliation de la Salette, a single wide space under an open wooden roof provides maximum space for worshippers, while the wide, high arcade would have allowed those seated in the aisles almost uninterrupted visibility. The nave canopy and north-facing altar, seen here, have recently been removed. [AA040129]*

dignified but above all economical to build. His first work in Liverpool was the handsome Church of St Vincent de Paul (1856–7) on St James' Street in the South End. In 1857 he designed the Church of the Holy Cross in Standish Street, replacing a temporary chapel established to serve the occupants of poor tenements. His town church design was perfected in the majestic Our Lady of Reconciliation de la Salette in Eldon Street (Figs 32 and 33) in the North End. The priest reached the church by a 'footbridge' linked to the west gallery, a reminder of the congested and unruly street that once separated church and presbytery.

Only in the decoration of some Catholic churches were the Liverpool poor afforded a glimpse of heaven. The splendid reredos and tabernacles of churches such as St Francis Xavier's, Sacred Heart and St Vincent de Paul's were designed to lift the eyes and the heart to heaven. In that relative latecomer to the North End, the Franciscan Friary Church of St Mary of the Angels in Fox Street (Pugin and Pugin, 1910), the impoverished worshippers were even afforded a glimpse of the glories of their Continental Catholic heritage. The church's patron was Amy Elizabeth Imrie, a Catholic convert and White Star shipping heiress who had become a nun of the Franciscan Order of Poor Clares. She filled the church, built in the Romanesque style, with treasures collected in Rome and Bologna (Fig 34).

Church attendance among Nonconformists was increasing in the mid-19th century, usually, it was feared, at the expense of the Church of England, although, dependent as they were on the income from pewrents, Nonconformist chapels had little choice but to follow congregations to better off neighbourhoods. An exception to this rule was the Toxteth Baptist Tabernacle on Park Road, built at the expense of the charismatic Scottish preacher William Peddie Lockhart (1835–93). Lockhart had begun his Liverpool preaching career at Hope Hall, which he rented on a weekly basis. He soon outgrew the venue and moved to the larger Hengler's Circus where he welcomed the American evangelist Dr Moody in 1867. In 1870 Lockhart raised over £7,000 from supporters. The foundation stone of the new chapel was laid by the famous Baptist evangelist Charles Spurgeon and opened on 20 October 1871, with seats for 2,000 (Fig 35). Although he was accused of not venturing into the very poorest of dockland areas, Lockhart claimed that six out of seven church members had not formerly attended any place of worship. The Tabernacle was considerably enlarged in 1882 and by 1886 Lockhart's stirring sermons were regularly attracting congregations of 1,500 people. Despite a troubled history in the 20th century, the Tabernacle has weathered the storms that have swept away many of its chapel neighbours, and its congregation, committed to the active service of one of Liverpool's poorest neighbourhoods, is growing.

Figure 34 (right) *The Baroque high altar of the Franciscan Friary Church of St Mary of the Angels, Fox Street, is said to have come from Bologna Cathedral, and Saints Charles Borromeo, Ignatius Loyola and Philip Neri are all reputed to have prayed before it. [AA035880]*

Figure 35 (above) *Toxteth Baptist Tabernacle, the only building by Liverpool architect W I Mason to survive intact, is a robust and quirky landmark on Park Road built in 1871 for Liverpool's most charismatic Baptist preacher, William Peddie Lockhart. [AA040975]*

A city fit for heroes?

The carnage of the First World War left an indelible mark on Liverpool congregations of all faiths and social classes. In common with towns and cities throughout Britain, Liverpool lost many thousands of men in the trenches of the western front, but the losses among its seafarers were also prodigious and the dockland neighbourhoods bore the brunt.

In the aftermath of the war the congregations of churches in some of Liverpool's poorest parishes continued to shrink as a consequence of slum clearance. This process, which had begun in the 1880s and 1890s, was given new impetus by the national commitment to make post-war Britain a country 'fit for heroes'. From 1925 Lancelot Keay implemented the Corporation's ambitious new housing programme. In search of land, the Corporation acquired sites adjoining Queen's Drive, taking the city up to and beyond the embrace of the great semicircular ring road first laid out in 1904.

In the city centre the impact of European Modernism was felt in the austere, clean lines of some of the blocks of walk-up flats. However, Liverpool was never entirely comfortable with Modernism, and in the acres of suburban social housing built in the inter-war years a domestic neo-Georgian style prevailed. It was in these new communities on the urban rim that churches and chapels were to have considerable impact in both architectural and social terms. The development of these estates, at Clubmoor and Norris Green, for example, was achieved in the teeth of the Great Depression. The evolution of the Speke estate, begun in 1938, was disrupted by the outbreak of the Second World War.

Brave new worlds?

Norris Green, begun in 1926, the largest and most successful of the Corporation's inter-war estates, was constructed on 650 acres of previously agricultural land to the east of Queen's Drive. Almost 8,000 houses were built, in units of varying size, and by 1932 it was home to 37,500 people. The street layout is regular and geometric, with a series of curving avenues, crescents and circles, in deliberate and striking contrast to the row-upon-row of straight streets with which many new Norris Green residents had been familiar. An efficient tram service was accommodated in the tree-lined centres of the main arterial roads. The estate was also provided with a variety of amenities – libraries, health centres, shops and schools. Charles Reilly, charismatic director of the Liverpool School of Architecture, warned against the visual monotony that might be a consequence of development on such a scale, and it was the churches and chapels that provided important architectural 'punctuation' within this predominantly domestic streetscape.

All church building had ceased during the First World War, but now new communities needed new churches and in 1927 Bishop Francis James Chavasse (1846–1928) launched the Bishop's Jubilee Building Campaign to raise money for new buildings ready to commemorate the 50th anniversary of the creation of the Anglican diocese in 1880. Norris Green, carved out of the parish of Fazakerley, was a beneficiary of the campaign. It was divided into two new districts, centred on Sedgemoor Road and Lorenzo Drive, served by the new churches of Christ Church (Ernest Gee, 1931–2, demolished 2006) and St Christopher (Bernard A Miller, 1930–2) respectively. For fund-raising purposes, Christ Church was designated the Bishop Chavasse Memorial Church, while St Christopher's was christened 'the Children's Church' and attracted the contributions of children throughout the diocese, who enrolled as knights and ladies of the Order of Jubilee Campaigners. Some local residents still recall the procession of costumed children who accompanied the bishop's procession from the railway station to St Christopher's for the laying of the foundation stone.

The churches of the 1930s were a showcase for the talents of a new generation of architects trained at the Liverpool School of Architecture, and Liverpool can boast a distinguished group of inter-war churches as a consequence. Charles Reilly, the school's director from 1904 to 1933, was at heart a champion of an American-influenced brand of Classicism that came to be termed 'the Liverpool manner', ideally suited to the public and commercial buildings of the city centre. The school's church specialists, Ernest Gee (Christ Church, Norris Green), Bernard Miller

(St Christopher's, Norris Green; St Columba's, Anfield, 1931–2; and St Aidan's, Speke, 1953) and Francis Xavier Velarde (the Catholic churches of St Matthew's, Clubmoor, 1927; St Monica's, Bootle, 1937; and the demolished St Alexander's, Bootle, 1956), on the other hand, were more eclectic in their approach to design. Blending Baroque, neo-Classicism and European Modernism, they were also sensitive to Byzantine and Romanesque models and, in common with other church architects of their generation, revered Early Christian buildings (Fig 36). Financial constraints resulted in a widespread reliance on brick and tile, but this necessity was turned into a virtue (Fig 37). In their angularity and severity these buildings invite comparison with cinemas and even power stations, but in the midst of so much that was low-rise and low-key, the churches represented architecture of distinction on a monumental scale.

Figure 38 *At St Christopher's, Norris Green, Bernard Miller used a plaster-coated steel frame to create the parabolic arches of its striking interior, quite unexpected from the severe angularity of its exterior. [DP034198]*

The inter-war churches are relatively conservative in their liturgical planning, but internally they are all exciting, creating seemingly vast uninterrupted spaces indebted to the round arch and expansive vault. Miller, in particular, experimented with new materials and techniques, at St Christopher's using a plaster-covered steel frame to create graceful parabolic arches quite unexpected from the solid rectilinear quality of the exterior. Velarde and Gee's Liverpool interiors are serious compared to the playful theatricality achieved by Miller, in which Staybright steel, mirror-glass and plywood are combined with the colourful decorative repertoire of the Jazz Age (Fig 38). These buildings had more in common with the 1930s picture palace than with Victorian ecclesiastical tradition. St Christopher's and St Monica's were among the first 20th-century buildings to be listed.

The architects worked with other Liverpool artists and craftsmen in order to provide their churches with distinguished decorations and furnishings. Exterior sculpture on the church hall of Christ Church, Norris Green, and on the west front of St Monica's, Bootle, and the Stations of the Cross at St Matthew's, Clubmoor (Fig 39), are by Herbert Tyson Smith, best known for the sculpture on the cenotaph on St George's plateau. Sculpture at St Christopher's and St Columba's is by Bainbridge Copnall, while painted altarpieces at St Columba's are the work of Mary Adshead.

The lives of the residents of the new inter-war estates were transformed in terms of comfort and convenience. However, in relocating families from their slum dwellings, the Corporation did not always replant original communities, so that many new Norris Green and Clubmoor residents found themselves socially at sea without the comfortable proximity of their old neighbours. Many residents felt keenly a sense of geographic isolation from the old life and neighbourhood in the city centre. In these circumstances, the role of the church in creating new social structures was essential, and many people depended on church membership for leisure and entertainment as well as spiritual well-being. This had been anticipated by the church planners, and Christ Church and St Christopher's, for example, were each at the centre of a small complex of buildings that included a

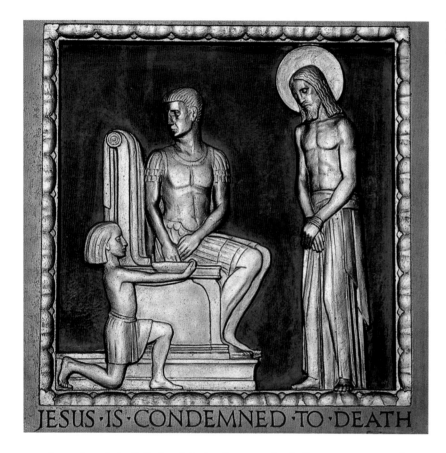

Figure 39 *'Jesus is condemned to Death', one of Herbert Tyson Smith's Stations of the Cross for St Matthew's, Clubmoor. [DP002396]*

spacious church hall. Indeed, in both cases, the hall was constructed ahead of the church. St Christopher's is also served by a small cloister linking the church and hall and enclosing a children's court overlooked by an outdoor pulpit (Fig 40). A successful parish centre added in 1998 now occupies the site of the unbuilt church hall intended for St Columba's, helping to secure the church's future at the centre of its community and providing local employment opportunities.

Gee, Miller and Velarde belonged to a generation of architects who believed in the power of architecture as an agent of social change. Despite the trauma of the First World War, it was still a world in which the church

Figure 40 *The children's cloister and outdoor pulpit of St Christopher's, Norris Green. Miller's simple Classical architecture is enriched with sculpture in pressed concrete by Bainbridge Copnall. [DP034197]*

was at the heart of society, and in the inter-war churches Liverpool's architects breathed new life into a much older concept of church and community. They also gave the council house residents of Liverpool's new estates exciting buildings to be proud of, and a lifetime later those that survive are still much loved by the people who worship in them.

CHAPTER 6

Cathedral ambitions

Liverpool became the seat of a bishop as soon as the Catholic episcopal hierarchy was re-established in England in 1850. Only in 1880 was the city's size and importance recognised by the creation of the Church of England bishopric, its territory carved out of the See of Chester, of which it had been part since the Reformation. From the outset, both new bishoprics made do with existing churches. The modest Catholic Church of St Nicholas, Copperas Hill, served as the pro-cathedral. In 1853 Edward Welby Pugin was commissioned to produce a design for a new cathedral in St Domingo Road in Everton. Work began in 1856 but only a Lady Chapel was built before the project was abandoned and the chapel became the parish church of Our Lady Immaculate. The dilapidated chapel was demolished in 1980. The Anglican bishop's pro-cathedral was established at St Peter's, in Church Street (*see* Fig 4). This arrangement was never considered satisfactory, and a lively debate as to the most appropriate site for a new cathedral ensued. St John's Gardens, in the shadow of St George's Hall, were canvassed for some time, and a design was prepared by William Emerson. In 1901 a more dramatic site on the ridge overlooking St James' Cemetery was finally selected. This ensured that the Anglican Cathedral dominated the city skyline.

From the portfolios of several hundred hopefuls, a shortlist of five architects was invited to submit a new design in 1903. The choice was made with the help of eminent assessors G F Bodley and Norman Shaw. The outcome was a surprise to the architectural establishment. Giles Gilbert Scott, while a member of one of the country's most illustrious architectural dynasties, was an untried architect of only 23 years of age. He was also a Roman Catholic. Until his death in 1907, Bodley was to be Scott's collaborator. Thereafter Scott had a free hand and the cathedral's construction was to be a lifetime commitment.

The Anglican Cathedral is England's last great Gothic Revival church, and Scott took full advantage of the drama afforded by the elevated rocky site, fulfilling Bishop Chavasse's requirement that the cathedral be visible above the city (Fig 41). The original design was for a cruciform church with a three-bay choir and six-bay nave. Two towers were positioned over the main transepts. Almost immediately Scott began to modify the design, reducing its fussy, spiky quality in favour of an

Construction of the third tier of the Catholic Cathedral, 1964. [Photography Mills Media Ltd]

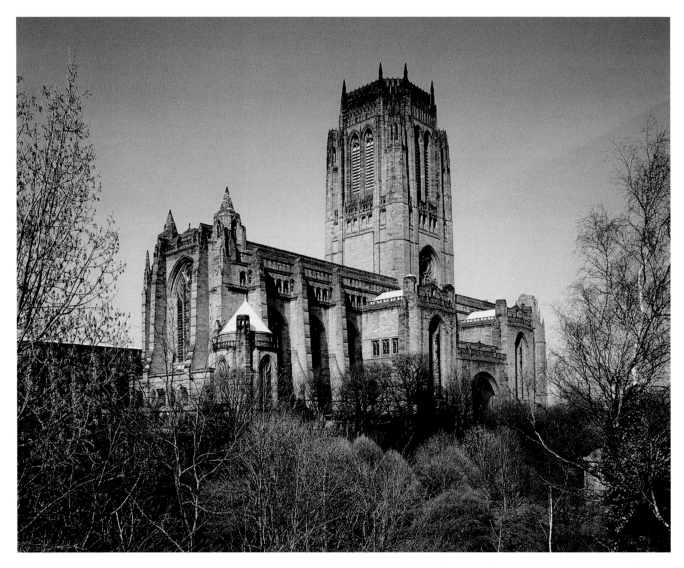

Figure 41 *The Anglican Cathedral, begun in 1904 and completed in 1978, England's last great Gothic church.* *[AA040753]*

Figure 42 (right) *The Lady Chapel of the Anglican Cathedral (looking east), the earliest part of the building to be completed.* *[AA040905]*

Figure 43 *A view from the central tower of the Anglican Cathedral into the eastern transepts and the chancel beyond. [AA040904]*

increasingly massive, simplified silhouette, already apparent in the second design of 1904. The rectangular Lady Chapel was positioned at the (ritual) south-east corner of the building, with a rectangular chapter house on the corresponding north-east angle. The Lady Chapel (Fig 42) was constructed quickly, opening in 1910. Not surprisingly, this is the part of the cathedral that displays Scott's greatest debt to Bodley in its refined and sophisticated interpretation of late medieval Gothic.

Even as the Lady Chapel was under construction, the design was undergoing the major revision that created the building we see today. Scott became increasingly free and inventive in his use of Gothic motifs, breathing new life into the medieval tradition. The pair of transeptal towers were abandoned in favour of a single massive central tower, positioned one bay further west. A second transept was positioned to the west of the tower, to balance its eastern counterpart. The space between the two transepts was employed to create two enormous porches, without medieval precedent, but majestic in scale and with added grandeur thanks to the programme of sculpture executed by Edward Carter Preston. The chapter house, reduced in size, became octagonal, creating a more dramatic outline at the north-east extremity of the site, linked to the choir by a passage. The relocation of the tower created the vast central space originally required of the design (Fig 43). Scott continued to make refinements to the design until his death in 1960, but the principal features of the building were now determined.

The choir and eastern transepts were complete by 1924, and the under-tower and western transepts by 1941. The last pinnacle of the tower was completed in 1942, by which time the Second World War was underway and Liverpool had become a major target of enemy action. The cathedral suffered bomb damage that destroyed most of the pre-war stained-glass windows. Progress on the nave had to wait for peace. It was begun in 1948 and completed in 1978, by which time the enthusiasm and optimism of the 1900s had evaporated and Liverpool was on the brink of a period of decline.

The brooding presence of the cathedral owes much to the dark Woolton sandstone from which it is built. Behind the scenes the cathedral is very much a modern building, employing brick and reinforced

Figure 44 *The 'Hallelujah door' in the Lady Chapel of the Anglican Cathedral exemplifies the superb quality of craftsmanship found throughout the cathedral.* [DP034202]

concrete and with a full range of modern services, including a lift. Its interior is a showcase for the finest in ecclesiastical craftsmanship (Fig 44): woodwork by Waring & Gillow, metalwork by the Bromsgrove Guild, sculpture by Edward Carter Preston, Walter Gilbert and Louis Weingartner, and stained glass by Burlison & Grylls, C E Kempe & Co, Morris & Co, James Powells & Sons (designed by J W Brown and James Hogan), Herbert Hendrie and Willie Wilson. The dramatic west window depicting Christ of the Trades, was designed and made by Carl Edwards.

Without a doubt, the most ambitious architectural project of the years between the wars was the construction of the new Metropolitan Cathedral of the Catholic archdiocese. The humble pro-Cathedral of St Nicholas was a reproach to the See, raised to Metropolitan status in 1911. In 1922 Richard Downey became archbishop and brought a new energy and determination to the scheme to build a cathedral worthy of the Northern Province. In 1930 the earlier sites were abandoned in favour of a prominent location on the top of Mount Pleasant and Brownlow Hill, the site of the former workhouse and within sight of the Anglican Cathedral already under construction. The new cathedral was intended to dwarf its Anglican counterpart in terms of size and grandeur. Indeed, had it been built according to plan, Downey's cathedral would have been the largest Catholic church in England, outstripping Westminster Cathedral. No competition was held, the project was simply awarded to Sir Edwin Lutyens (1869–1944), the pre-eminent architect of the day, a man at the height of his powers. The scale of his ambition is recorded in numerous drawings and in a magnificent scale model (Fig 45), in the tradition of Wren's models of St Paul's Cathedral.

Figure 45 *The scale model of Sir Edwin Lutyens' original concept for a new Catholic Cathedral, now in the Walker Art Gallery. [National Museums Liverpool, Walker Art Gallery]*

Lutyens' ecclesiastical colossus was intended to combine the styles of
Rome, Byzantium and Romanesque Christendom, an eclectic hybrid of
astonishing ambition. A short, double-aisled nave with doubled-aisled
transepts and a short apsidal chancel would be entered through a façade
in the form of a triumphal arch. A dome 155m high, taller than that of St
Peter's in Rome, would stand above the crossing. The cathedral was to
rest on a dramatic and cavernous crypt (Fig 46). In his choice of
materials – brick with granite dressings – Lutyens put his trust in the

Figure 46 *Lutyens' crypt of the Catholic Cathedral, all
that was built before the outbreak of the Second World
War. [Conway Library, The Courtauld Institute of Art,
London]*

bricklaying skills of Liverpool craftsmen, honed to perfection over generations in the city's docks and warehouses. That his faith was well placed can be seen in the extraordinary quality of the crypt, begun in 1933 and completed by the time war broke out in 1939.

In the difficult years after the war, Lutyens' great leviathan was abandoned, as resources were limited and the reconstruction of Blitzed homes took precedence over the building of a cathedral. Both Lutyens and Archbishop Downey were dead and it was only in 1959, under Archbishop (subsequently Cardinal) J C Heenan, that the cathedral project was resurrected, albeit on a more modest scale. Notwithstanding, Liverpool's new Metropolitan Cathedral was not only the most important Catholic project of the post-war period, it has also proved to be an iconic expression of the aspirations of the Liturgical Movement that was breathing new life into liturgy and worship and having a major impact on church design in the 20th century.

At the heart of the Liturgical Movement was a renewed focus on the importance of the Eucharist, something it shared with the Oxford Movement. But it was also a movement in which the active participation of the whole body of the Church was promoted, with an enhanced role for the laity. The Eucharist was transformed into a corporate act and so needed to be visible and physically accessible. In architectural terms this was expressed by the move towards integrated single spaces, with the altar brought forward into the church, or better still, placed at the heart of a centrally planned space. Choir screens were abandoned and choirs, formerly accommodated in choir stalls at the front of the church, were moved to western galleries, where they no longer obstructed the sight of the altar. In pre-war England the opportunities for experimentation were relatively limited, although in the 1930s some priests and architects were advocating change. The priest and architectural writer Peter Hammond was the most articulate advocate of a new kind of church architecture, and a number of new churches built before the Second World War, many for Catholic congregations, were centrally planned around an accessible altar. The Second Vatican Council, convened by Pope John XXIII in 1962, was to be a watershed event in which the Roman Catholic Church sought to engage with the modern world. As a consequence of the resultant Decree on the Liturgy, Latin was replaced by the vernacular as the language of the Mass and greater lay participation was encouraged. From 1964, the altar of all new churches was to be brought forward from the east wall of the church to allow the priest to face the congregation during the celebration of the Eucharist.

Having taken the momentous decision to abandon the ambitious Lutyens cathedral concept, even in its scaled-down version, Archbishop Heenan launched a competition for a new design, for an affordable and achievable building to accommodate 3,000 worshippers, a church to be as much 'of its time' as Archbishop Downey had intended the Lutyens cathedral to be. Applicants to the competition (there were nearly 300 submissions in total) received a letter from the archbishop that made clear his over-riding liturgical priority: 'The High Altar is the central feature of every Catholic church. It must be the focus of the new building. The trend of the liturgy is to associate the congregation ever more closely with the celebrant of the Mass … . The attention of all who enter should be arrested and held by the altar.' Frederick Gibberd, winner of the competition, succeeded spectacularly in expressing Heenan's vision (Fig 47). His circular church, 59.4m in diameter, has the high altar at its heart, surrounded by 13 chapels. The whole is crowned by a spiky, brilliantly glazed corona, recalling that this is the Cathedral of Christ the King. The building was innovative in its use of materials, its skeleton formed of boomerang-shaped concrete trusses tied together by ring beams at two levels. Flying buttresses carry thrust to the ground. The corona glazing, designed by John Piper and fabricated by Patrick Reyntiens, is an abstract construction of *dalles de verre* held in resin. The architectural brief stipulated that the new cathedral should incorporate the Lutyens crypt. Gibberd transformed the roof of the crypt into a piazza, extended to the south to form the podium on which his new church now rests. The cathedral and the piazza is now approached via a sweep of broad steps, created in 2003 by Falconer Chester (Fig 48), and the principal entrance is through the base of the wedge-shaped bell-tower, the bells hung in openings at the apex. Even the main doors are uncompromisingly modern – sliding fibreglass, decorated with expressionistic symbols of the Four Evangelists by William Mitchell (Fig 49).

Figure 47 *The interior of Sir Frederick Gibberd's centrally planned Catholic Cathedral. [DP002413]*

Figure 48 (left) *The distinctive exterior and campanile, its crown-like architectural shape expressing the dedication of the Catholic Cathedral to Christ the King. [DP034205]*

Figure 49 *Monumental fibreglass doors with symbols of the Four Evangelists, by William Mitchell. [DP034206]*

The interior is a showcase for equally dramatic 1960s abstract artworks, easily distinguished from the more traditional and figurative additions of more recent years. Stained glass, designed by Margaret Traherne and Ceri Richards (also responsible for the abstract reredos in the Blessed Sacrament Chapel), plays an important role in the subsidiary chapels and frames their entrances. The high altar, a single free-standing block of white marble, is lit by a downpour of light and colour from the corona, and is crowned with an angular baldachin of aluminium rods designed by Gibberd himself. The congregation is accommodated in concentric rows of curved benches, the whole community thus afforded an unimpeded view of the altar.

The cathedral was built with astonishing speed – between 1962 and 1967 – and has suffered from structural problems addressed in recent repairs by Vis Williams Prichard with funding from English Heritage. The original external mosaic cladding, for example, has been replaced with a cladding of glass-reinforced plastic, while the conical roof, originally covered in aluminium, has been refurbished in stainless steel.

Both cathedrals have had an impact on their surroundings and have become a force for regeneration. Scott's original scheme for housing in a cathedral precinct was not realised, but in 1982 the area occupied by late Georgian and Victorian terraced housing was redeveloped in a scheme of town houses (by Brook Carmichael Associates) and landscaping (by Derek Lovejoy and Partners). In 2003, as part of a scheme that included the restoration of Lutyens' crypt, a welcoming piazza surrounding the Catholic Cathedral was created, with new triumphal staircase, restaurant and visitor centre. Both cathedrals have reclaimed the enthusiasm and optimism of their founders and – refurbished and re-equipped – are ready to serve the worshippers, visitors and pilgrims of the new millennium.

CHAPTER 7

A single city of many nations

By the end of the 19th century Liverpool had become a truly cosmopolitan city, second only to London as capital of trade and commerce. Many immigrant communities were in more or less permanent residence, and many more itinerant seamen passed through the port, many of them from West Africa or the Far East. Some immigrant communities prospered and have left their architectural mark. The fortunes of others have waxed and waned. Their places of worship were often temporary, modest or taken over from others. Many have disappeared leaving almost no trace.

Passing through

Chapels for seamen were among the most ephemeral of structures. Some were established on hulks moored in the dock. 'The Mariners' Church' moored at the south end of George's Dock, for example, was capable of seating 1,000 worshippers, but writing in 1866 *The Porcupine* reported that 'going to the Mariners' Church in search of sailors is something like going to St Martin's in the Fields looking for daisies'. It sank in 1876. Rather more popular were the seamen's missions, including the Sailors' Home and the North and South Bethels. Concern for the spiritual welfare of seamen was matched by anxiety about their moral welfare and physical well-being while ashore. Idleness and vice were combated by non-alcoholic refreshment, games and reading rooms, wholesome alternatives to Liverpool's thousands of pubs. *The Porcupine's* reporter found these missions to be far better attended, despite the poor quality of the religious services conducted there!

Many seafarers passing through or with only insecure rights to reside in Liverpool found themselves marginalised and discriminated against in religion as in every other aspect of their lives ashore. Most black and Asian people lived in the South End in some of the poorest housing in the city. A Wesleyan African Mission was established in 1923 in Templar Hall in Mill Street, while the African Churches Mission, founded in 1931 in two houses in Hill Street (Fig 50), run by the Nigerian-born Pastor George Daniels Ekarte, received the support of the Anglican Bishop of

The German Church, at the junction of Canning Square and Bedford Street North. [AA045458]

Liverpool. The mission closed in 1964 and has disappeared as a result of extensive redevelopment of the tightly packed terraces of the Dingle.

Baltic trade, although eclipsed by trade with America, was of long-standing importance to Liverpool. Services for German seamen were conducted in St Michael's, Upper Pitt Street, and a German Evangelical Lutheran community acquired Newington Chapel in Renshaw Street in 1871. The congregation moved to Canning Street in 1931, where its building was a casualty of the Blitz. A modest modern building was constructed after the war (*see* page 66). A far more distinguished building is the Gustav Adolfs Kyrka, or Swedish Seamen's Church (now the Scandinavian Seamen's Church), on Park Road. By the mid-1850s over 50,000 Swedish seamen were said to be visiting Liverpool annually. In 1883 W D Caroë, then a young member of J L Pearson's architectural practice, was commissioned to design a new church. The Caroë family

Figure 50 *Pastor Ekarte's African Churches Mission at 122–4 Hill Street, Toxteth. [National Museums Liverpool, [National Museums Liverpool, Merseyside Maritime Museum]*

Figure 51 *With its dramatic and bristling roof line and striking lead-covered spire, W D Caroë's Gustav Adolfs Kyrka is one of Liverpool's most memorable and eye-catching churches. [AA040906]*

lived at Blundellsands and Caroë's father was the Danish consul in Liverpool, so the family had Scandinavian connections. Although the influence of the massing of Pearson's Liverpool masterpiece, St Agnes's, Ullet Road (*see* pp 22–3), is recognisable in the Gustav Adolfs Kyrka, the building is undeniably evocative of Swedish architectural styles (Fig 51).

The church, tightly packed on a small site (Fig 52), was but one component in a multi-purpose building. A reading room and recreational facilities are located beneath the church, and the minister's house, which is

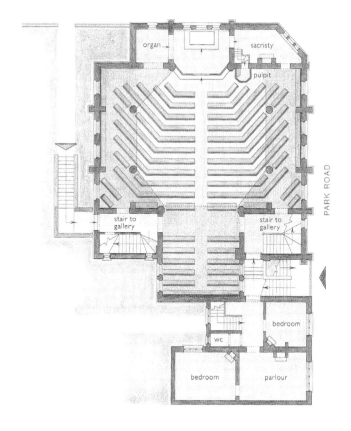

Figure 52 *The original plan of the Gustav Adolfs Kyrka. [Redrawn from contemporary publications]*

also the consulate, adjoins the church at its south-west corner. During the Second World War, many Scandinavian seamen found themselves unable to return to their Nazi-occupied homeland and relied on the church for support. Many put down roots and became Liverpool residents by default. The church was reordered in the 1960s, when a mezzanine floor was inserted and its original galleries were removed. Despite the subdivision of the worship space, the church remains impressive under its steeply pitched octagonal roof and was repaired and sympathetically redecorated in 1991. The alterations were designed to create smaller, flexible spaces for the programme of social services that continue to be offered to the Scandinavian residents of Merseyside. The ministers serve the older expatriates, in addition to making regular visits to the vessels passing through the nearby port. A sizable Scandinavian student population attending Liverpool's two universities has provided the church with a significant new congregation although the withdrawal of support from Sweden places the future of this remarkable church in the balance.

Putting down roots

The years between 1800 and 1850 saw Liverpool's indigenous population swelled by the growing tide of immigration. Irish migrants first arrived in Liverpool in significant numbers in the closing decades of the 18th century and although by no means all were Catholic, their arrival did not go unnoticed by the more extreme Protestants in the town. The steady trickle became a flood as a consequence of the potato famine during the 1840s, resulting in the enormous growth in Liverpool's Catholic population. In terms of their social class (most were unskilled agricultural labourers), educational background (many were illiterate) and language (many were Gaelic speakers), these destitute new arrivals must have seemed just as alien as immigrants from Continental Europe. A sometimes ugly sectarianism is a thread that runs through Liverpool's 19th-century history. Although extreme Protestant antipathy to Catholicism became more pronounced in the famine years, a riot between Orangemen and Irish Catholics had already taken place on 12

July 1819 – the anniversary of the Battle of the Boyne – for while the majority of migrants may have been Roman Catholic, Liverpool was also home to a significant number of Ulster Protestants. The number of Orange Lodges in Liverpool was only exceeded by those in Belfast. The 12 July and 17 March (St Patrick's Day) parades were consequently potential flashpoints for violence throughout the century.

The splendid Catholic Church of St Patrick on Park Place (1821–7, Fig 53) was to be one of the most contentious buildings of the period.

Figure 53 *St Patrick's, Park Place, unambiguously associated with Irish Catholicism by the addition of a life-size statue of St Patrick to its west front. Successive attempts by Orangemen to pull the figure down were unsuccessful. [AA040968]*

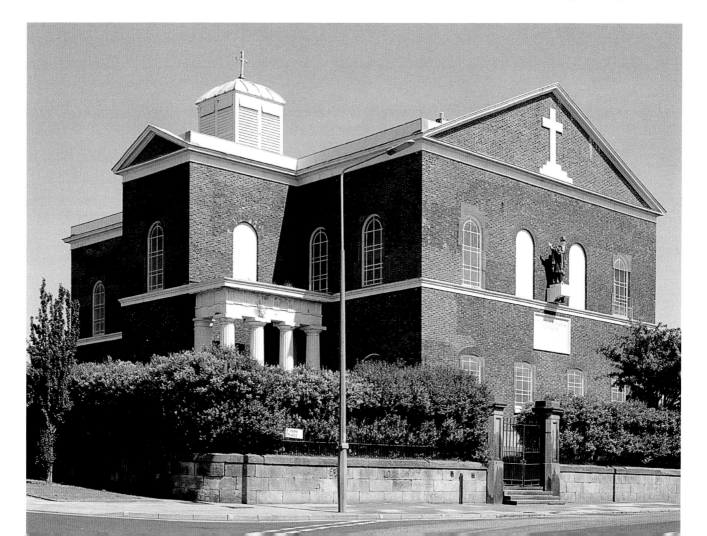

Although public worship had been legal since 1791, St Patrick's was a building project on a scale hitherto unprecedented in Liverpool. From the outset, the church was closely associated with the Irish community, already a significant component of the town's Catholic population. The men of the 88th Regiment of the Connaught Rangers are said to have contributed a day's pay to the fabric fund and a portion of specially blessed shamrock was buried in the foundations, laid in 1821. John Slater's Grecian cross plan provided ample accommodation, much of it for the poor. In a reversal of arrangements that applied in many Anglican churches and Nonconformist chapels of the period, the plentiful ground floor seating was free, with smaller numbers of rented seats at gallery level. The church opened in 1827 amidst great celebration.

Nineteenth-century Liverpool also boasted chapels to serve the increasingly important Welsh and Scottish communities. A Welsh Calvinist Methodist Chapel was built in Pall Mall in 1787, serving the fast-growing community of Welsh-speaking Anglesey masons and quarrymen attracted to Liverpool by the rapid expansion of the town. By 1813 it was estimated that 8,000 Welsh men and women lived in Liverpool, a figure that had risen tenfold by the end of the century. As the 19th-century building boom continued, Liverpool came to be called 'the capital of North Wales'. Welsh migrants tended to be more highly skilled than their Irish counterparts although, like many Irish, they were set apart by their language. Welsh life and culture in Liverpool was focused on, and indeed fostered by, the chapel, which provided recreation and education as well as spiritual sustenance. Of the scores of Welsh chapels once active in Liverpool, few remain in use. The Victoria Chapel in Crosshall Street, designed in 1878 by J A Picton for Welsh Calvinist Methodists, has been converted and until recently has been used by the juvenile courts, while the Welsh Calvinist Methodist Chapel in Chatham Street (Oliver and Lamb, 1860–1) survives as a façade, fronting the University of Liverpool Management School, completed in 2002. The greatest architectural monument to Welsh nonconformity, the Welsh Presbyterian Church in Princes Road, is described on pages 24–5. Even the Church of England made provision for Welsh speakers, for example at St Deniol's, Upper Parliament Street of 1894, which survives as a furniture warehouse. Once

Figure 54 *St Andrew's Scottish Presbyterian Church on Rodney Street, photographed in 1975 before the 1983 fire that almost destroyed it.* [BB75/5593]

the influx of new Welsh-speakers began to diminish by the end of the 19th century, the cultural and linguistic distinctiveness of the community was undermined. Intermarriage and social mobility have also taken their toll. The Heathfield Road Welsh Presbyterian Chapel, Smithdown Place (R Owen & Son, 1924–7), is now the sole surviving Welsh chapel of note in a city that once hosted an Eisteddfod.

Liverpool's Scottish Presbyterians first worshipped in Oldham Street Chapel, built in 1793 to serve a community over 9,000 strong by 1851. Their most important architectural monument in Liverpool is St Andrew's Scottish Presbyterian Church (1823–4) in Rodney Street (Fig 54). This unremarkable two-storey brick box designed by the church committee was transformed by its monumental Greek Revival façade designed by John Foster Junior, recalling the Grecian travels of his youth. St Andrew's marked the architectural high-water mark of Liverpool's Scottish community. The northern tower was dismantled following a

Figure 55 *Russell Street Great Synagogue was established in 1901 for an Orthodox Ashkenazi congregation of immigrants from Eastern Europe in a former Nonconformist chapel. [Liverpool Record Office, Liverpool Libraries]*

disastrous fire in 1983 and the church is now a building at risk, awaiting a viable scheme to secure the future of this Rodney Street landmark.

New wine in old vessels

Immigration, linguistic differences and distinctive traditions of worship also account for the proliferation of synagogues in Liverpool in the years around 1900. Intolerance and persecution of Jews in the Russian Empire in the period 1870–90 prompted a westwards exodus. While tens of thousands were trans-migrants en route to the United States, many stayed to make Liverpool their home. The indigenous anglicised Jewish community provided generous charity, but had little in common with their co-religionists from Eastern Europe. Writing in 1899, B L Benas, historian of Liverpool Jewry, described the services of the newcomers, 'full of emphatic, vivid, even uncouth, devotion … the weird swinging of their bodies during their orisons' and 'their hearty unison in songs of praise'.[6] The immigrants found the anglicised ways and worship of Liverpool Jewry equally alien and preferred to establish their own places of worship. With limited resources, the new arrivals took over buildings vacated by some of Liverpool's declining Christian congregations. The Claremont Grove Chapel in Fountains Road, for example, built for Nonconformists c1820, and taken over by Catholics in 1871, became Kirkdale Synagogue in 1888. The New Beth Hamedresh opened in a former Nonconformist chapel in Brownlow Hill in 1896, moving to the Central Synagogue in Islington in 1908, while the Great Synagogue in Russell Street (Fig 55) took over another disused Nonconformist chapel in 1901. By 1914 immigrants had founded 6 synagogues and at least 15 *chevroth* (conventicles) were dotted around the inner city.

This process of recycling has continued and has benefited immigrant faith communities even more recently established in Liverpool, particularly those associated with the south Asian subcontinent. Indians are recorded as having settled in Liverpool by the late 1860s, although no record of their religious affiliation survives. In the period before the Second World War, a small number arrived from the North-West Frontier Province and the Punjab area of pre-partition India. The upheavals of

Figure 56 *The assembled* murtis *(deities) of the Shree Radha Krishna Mandir, occupying a former Welsh Presbyterian Chapel on Edge Lane. [AA041307]*

partition encouraged more people to seek a new life in England and many members of Liverpool's Sikh and Hindu communities have family roots in this area.

Liverpool's Hindus and Sikhs have had few difficulties in taking on and converting the surplus buildings vacated by Christian congregations. The focus of Hindu worship and community life in Liverpool is the Shree Radha Krishna Mandir and Hindu Cultural Organisation in Edge Lane (Fig 56), on the edge of Kensington, another area undergoing urban regeneration. The mandir occupies what was originally the hall of a Welsh Presbyterian Chapel built in 1899, while, in a reversal of fortunes, the adjoining former church is now used for community and social activities. The mandir serves Hindus in Liverpool and from further afield, in Merseyside and North Wales. Connections with India remain strong, not least in terms of the decoration of the mandir's interior. The main worship space is decorated with a series of spectacular canvases depicting religious and historical scenes, executed by visiting Indian artists who resided in Liverpool for the duration of the commission. The *murtis* (statues of deities) occupying the shrine platform were all carved in India and express a devotional diversity that would be unusual in a mandir of comparable size in India – a reflection of the varied geographic origins of the Liverpool community.

The Sikh community occupies the 1904 Grade II–listed former Wellington Road Methodist Church, while Methodists continue to worship in the smaller church hall immediately adjoining, a good example of how the passage of a historic building from one faith group to another can result in a sustainable future for both.

England's first mosque

In 1889 a mosque was established at 8 Brougham Terrace by Manx-born solicitor and Muslim convert William Henry Quilliam, better known as Sheik Abdullah Quilliam (1851–1932). Although most of Liverpool's Muslims were itinerant seamen from overseas, the mosque's founder and many of its worshippers were relatively well-to-do English converts. In

Figure 57 *The only known photograph of the interior of the Mosque and Muslim Institute at 8 Brougham Terrace. This is probably the 'Saracenic' lecture hall of 1895. [Liverpool Record Office, Liverpool Libraries. From JH McGovern* Lectures on Saracenic Architecture *(Liverpool, 1896–8) H726.2 MACG]*

1895 architect J H McGovern altered the building in a 'Saracenic style' (Fig 57) and drew up plans, which came to naught, for a new purpose-built mosque to be built in Geneva Road. Nothing survives of the mosque interior, although it is commemorated by a plaque on the exterior. With the support of the Bishop of Liverpool, the Abdullah Quilliam Society and Liverpool's Muslim community have launched an ambitious fund-raising campaign aimed at restoring this immensely important monument to Islam in Britain.

Before the Second World War the streets nearest the south docks, such as Upper Pitt Street and Stanhope Street, and the Parliament Street and Granby Street area had been at the heart of Liverpool's black, Chinese and Asian communities. The bomb damage to this dockside area was extensive and prompted something of an exodus of families into the Granby area of Toxteth, where large houses vacated by their prosperous middle-class residents could be subdivided to accommodate many families. By the early 1970s Granby Street had a dozen shops run by Yemeni traders and was popularly known as 'the street of the Arabs'.

Following the closure of the mosque built by Abdullah Quilliam, Muslims in Liverpool met for Friday prayers in private homes, notably in the Hatherley Street home of Yemeni seaman Ali Hazzan and in the Pitt Street home of Mir Alam, who had emigrated to England from the North-West Frontier Province in 1919. The Liverpool Muslim Society was founded in 1953 and in 1958 acquired a site in Hatherley Street on land formerly occupied by terraced housing. The Al-Rahma Mosque (Fig 58) was created largely through the efforts of Yemeni and Pakistani residents of the area, a Muslim community swelled by the arrival of Somalis from the 1980s onwards. For Muslim communities the adaptation of a disused church or chapel is seldom satisfactory, as the accurate orientation of the building towards Makkah is critical. After protracted delays, the foundation stone was laid in 1965. The building continues to evolve as the community matures and new resources are found.

Figure 58 *Al-Rahma Mosque, Hatherley Street, the heart of Liverpool's present-day Muslim community. [DP034180]*

CHAPTER 8

Facing the future

The special character of Liverpool owes much to the buildings erected as an expression of faith. From the medieval Church of All Saints, Childwall, and the Ancient Chapel of Toxteth, which were both once at the centre of village communities, to the two great 20th-century cathedrals that crown the ridge high above the river, places of worship are powerful symbols of the city's rich heritage. Within the city today there are 85 listed places of worship, whilst many others, though unlisted, give a sense of place to the neighbourhoods within which they stand. Yet an increasing number of these cherished buildings are under threat, and without the tireless efforts of the dwindling number of committed individuals who care for them, their future would be bleak.

The present-day surplus of religious buildings in the city owes much to the population explosion of the 19th and early 20th centuries, when Liverpool was the second port of the British Empire. Churches and chapels sprung up to serve the huge influx of migrant workers and their families who moved into the inner core and urban fringe of the city at this time. Even though many places of worship disappeared in the 20th century in the face of commercial pressures, recent depopulation and dispersal of communities has left the city today with a much greater number of religious buildings than it can sustain. The problem is also compounded by the fact that the churches that remain in the once densely populated inner suburbs no longer serve the areas where people choose to live. Now that the city's economy is expanding, and business confidence has revived, people are starting to return to the city centre once again. Yet this welcome upturn is unlikely to halt the continued decline in attendance at traditional religious services, nor to prevent further closures as the process of rationalisation by religious organisations takes effect in the face of increased economic and administrative pressures.

What then is the future for these cherished buildings, and how best can they be preserved? Experience has shown that keeping them in use for worship offers the best prospect: it is the purpose for which they were built. Should worship cease, other suitable uses are not always easy to find. Yet, where a building has an uncertain future solely as a place of worship, the first priority must be to explore how it might play a more active role within the neighbourhood. For if the wider community is

The Ark, the New Hebrew Congregation Synagogue, Greenbank Drive. [AA030490]

involved, more people will use the building, thus encouraging a shared sense of ownership and a wider responsibility for its upkeep.

Increased community use may of course require change, but this is nothing to be afraid of, for adaptation of buildings is part of a long tradition. Churches have been altered or improved by every generation throughout history, reflecting changing patterns of worship, differing aesthetic taste, or a need for new facilities. In the medieval and Georgian periods, Anglican churches were often centres of the community, where justice was dispensed, education took place and local meetings were held. Our present-day reticence about using churches for secular purposes dates only from the mid-19th century, and whilst the majority of Liverpool's places of worship were built after this change in religious sensibility took effect, most are nonetheless well suited to accommodate the range of functions that modern-day communities demand. Although care must always be exercised in adapting such buildings, there are many ways in which changes can be made without harming the special character of the place.

Some churches, for example, have an undercroft that can be operated quite independently from the main worship space. This might provide income for the maintenance of the building, as with the crypt at the Catholic Cathedral, which is used for concerts, dinners, dances and undergraduate examinations. The space below a tower can often be screened off to accommodate a lavatory or kitchen. Where there are galleries, the area underneath might be suitable for conversion to meeting rooms, daycare and drop-in facilities, or even a café. A good example of shared usage is St Bride's Church, Catherine Street (Fig 59), where a series of offices for charitable and voluntary organisations is accommodated within screened enclosures below the galleries, leaving the central area free for worship. Where galleries do not exist, it may still be possible to design ancillary spaces at the end of an aisle or another little used area of the interior. More radical solutions may also be possible, as demonstrated by successful examples found elsewhere in the UK involving the introduction of modern galleries or enclosed structures within the aisles, or even the subdivision of the nave to form multi-storey accommodation at the west end.

Figure 59 *The interior of St Bride's Church, Catherine Street, with office accommodation for charitable and volunteer organisations inserted unobtrusively under the galleries. [Sarah Brown]*

Figure 60 *Sacred Heart, Hall Lane, with its sumptuous Pugin and Pugin high altar of 1891 untouched by the introduction of a forward altar platform. [DP034179]*

Alterations may also result from a desire to introduce new patterns of worship. Often changes involve moving fittings such as pulpits or fonts, rearrangement of chancels and sanctuaries, or the creation of a nave altar in order to bring the celebration of the sacraments closer to the worshippers. Generally such changes can be accommodated without serious detriment to the special character of the building. However, such changes require special care in the case of Roman Catholic churches and of Anglican churches designed on Tractarian principles, with chancel screens, choir stalls and richly decorated wall surfaces. It is generally preferable to introduce a nave altar and platform, leaving the east end unaltered; a good example of this being the Church of the Sacred Heart, Hall Lane (Fig 60), where the high altar and the spectacular alabaster reredos remain the focal point.

Alongside adaptations due to liturgical reform, there is an understandable desire for better comfort and convenience. Greater energy efficiency and sustainability are also major contributors to change. Today people expect that public spaces should have effective heating systems, be well lit and be equipped with comfortable seating. In the case of heating and lighting, there may be many different ways of servicing the building, but the best solution will depend on expert opinion. Where a rigid arrangement of fixed pews hampers flexibility or causes discomfort, their removal may be an option, though in the case of high-quality seating that is contemporary with the church, or part of a significant historic reordering scheme, the scope for modification may be more limited. Lavatory and tea-making facilities are needed in most places of worship today, and they should always be conveniently located within or attached to the main part of the building.

In spite of the adaptability of most of Liverpool's historic places of worship, few reordering schemes can be singled out as examples of good practice. Fortunately, one particularly unsuitable scheme, at the Church of Our Lady of Reconciliation de la Salette, Eldon Street Vauxhall (*see* Fig 33), involving the introduction of a suspended ceiling and reorientation of the direction of worship to focus on the south wall of the nave, has recently been reversed. In contrast, the treatment of St Mary's, Edge Hill (Fig 61), demonstrates how an interior can be

gradually yet sensitively adapted over time. Designed as a simple preaching box, this church was given choir stalls in the early 20th century. In 1958 a nave platform and a wooden communion table were introduced; then later the west end below the gallery was screened off to provide a parish room. Despite the removal of some of the box pews, the essential character of the simple galleried interior remains unharmed.

Figure 61 *St Mary's, Edge Hill, built with only a shallow sanctuary in 1812–13, with altar rails and choir stalls added c1913 and a nave platform of 1958. [Sarah Brown]*

Figure 62 *The austere but elegant parish room added in 2004 at the east end of the Church of St Anthony of Egypt, Scotland Road, designed by John Pritchard of Pritchard Williams of Liverpool. [DP034201]*

Placing new facilities within an existing building is generally more convenient and avoids the difficulties that can occur with extensions. In some cases, however, there may little scope for adaptation and an addition is the only solution. The most ambitious example in Liverpool is probably the large extension at the west end of St Peter's, Woolton, where a glass screen separates the Victorian church interior from the new parish hall. Another option is to place new facilities in a detached building. Whilst this may involve some inconvenience, it can have advantages in terms of flexibility as well as cost, since it avoids the constraints of adding to a listed building. At the Church of St Anthony of Egypt, Scotland Road (Fig 62), the simple flat-roofed parish room and interpretation centre does not look out of place alongside the east end of the elaborate Gothic revival church

Under the terms of the Disability Discrimination Act, places of worship must be accessible for people with disabilities. This means finding alternative ways of providing access. The legislation, however, does not override existing secular or ecclesiastical laws relating to historic buildings, and making physical alterations to the building may not be the only solution. The best approach is to start with an access audit and then to ensure that all changes take account of the character of the building as well as the needs of its users.

Places of worship are generally complex and expensive buildings to repair and maintain. In Liverpool the majority were built in the 19th and early 20th centuries, and are now reaching an age where major investment in their basic structure is required. Roofs may need reslating, the stonework of towers and spires may be crumbling, leadwork is wearing thin, rainwater goods may have rusted, and stained glass windows buckled. If water is allowed to penetrate the fabric, dry rot may well take hold, whilst plasterwork, wall paintings or coloured decoration can be damaged. Many parishes cannot afford the costs of major repairs and so the work gets put off, causing greater deterioration and spiralling costs. In some cases well-meaning volunteers have carried out inappropriate repairs which have done more harm than good. To assist with urgent repairs, grants are available from English Heritage and the Heritage Lottery Fund under the *Repair Grant for Places of Worship* scheme. Many listed buildings in Liverpool have benefited under this

scheme, including the churches of St Paul, Stoneycroft; St John the
Baptist, Tuebrook; St Christopher, Norris Green; St Philip Neri,
Catherine Street; and St Margaret's of Antioch, Princes Road; the Old
Hebrew Congregation Synagogue and the Greek Orthodox Church of
St Nicholas, also both on Princes Road. The two cathedrals have also
received substantial assistance under a separate English Heritage scheme.

The demand for grant aid, however, greatly exceeds the funds
available and can only be awarded for urgent works. It is therefore critical
that regular maintenance takes place – replacing slipped slates, clearing
leaves from gutters and checking the drains – so as to avoid huge repair
bills mounting up in the future. Few congregations have the specialist
skills needed to look after a complex historic building, and often they do
not know where to turn to for help. It is important that they receive the
right support from faith or denominational organisations, including
training initiatives, assistance with project development, and perhaps
grant or loan support. At the appropriate stage there may be a need for
discussions with English Heritage.

What happens if worship ceases and the building becomes
redundant? In the case of listed buildings, regulations are in place to try
and find a way of preserving the building. On rare occasions important
Anglican churches can be transferred to the Churches Conservation
Trust, which receives funding from government and the Church
Commissioners (in Liverpool the Trust currently cares for the Church of
St James, St James Place, Toxteth). Redundant and threatened non-
Anglican places of worship of outstanding interest may similarly be taken
into care by The Historic Chapels Trust. In most instances, however,
efforts are made to find alternative uses. For example appropriate new
uses for the New Hebrew Congregation Synagogue in Greenbank Drive
(Ernest Alfred Shennan, 1936–7), one of the best 1930s synagogues in
the country and recently relisted at Grade II*, are currently under
discussion.

In Liverpool a number of places of worship have found more or less
sympathetic new uses, thus avoiding demolition. The former Victoria
Chapel in Crosshall Street is used as juvenile courts. The Welsh Calvinist
Methodist Church on Chatham Street is used as teaching

Figure 63 *Alma de Cuba, a fashionable restaurant now occupying the former St Peter's Church in up-and-coming Seel Street. [Martin Stewart]*

accommodation by the University of Liverpool. Methodist Central Hall, Renshaw Street, contains a bizarre mix of bars and second-hand clothes stalls. St Peter's, Seel Street, the oldest surviving Catholic church in the city, has been transformed with theatrical flair into a fashionable restaurant (Fig 63). Rock climbers now exercise their skills on the 'Awesome Walls' of St Alban's, Athol Street (Fig 64). The Strict Baptist Chapel in Shaw Street has been subdivided to form apartments. The Franciscan Friary Church of St Mary of the Angels, Fox Street, with its fine Italian Baroque fittings, is now used as a rehearsal space for the Royal Liverpool Philharmonic Orchestra.

Yet for the communities that are affected by the closure of places of worship in Liverpool, such losses sever tangible connections with the past. Therefore it cannot simply be left to those with a direct responsibility for their upkeep to ensure their continued survival. All of us with a responsibility for the regeneration of the city and the creation of sustainable communities must work together. The essential appeal of these buildings depends on their continued use for worship, but they will have a much more secure and sustainable future if the wider community becomes actively engaged.

Figure 64 *Awesome Walls, Liverpool's popular climbing centre, a light-touch adaptation of the former Church of St Alban, Athol Street. [DP034191]*

Notes

1 Picton 1883, 196

2 Picton 1875 Vol I, 146

3 Picton 1875, Vol II, 487

4 The architects' description, quoted in *The Liverpool Old Hebrew Congregation, Princes Road Synagogue Order of the Jubilee Service*, 21 Sept 1921, 17 (Liverpool Record Office H296.1.PRI.)

5 Kadish 2006, 135

6 Benas 1899, 83

References and further reading

Amos, Francis J C 1968 *Places of Worship in Liverpool. A Study of their Organisation and Distribution.* Liverpool: City Planning Office

Benas, B L 1899 'Records of the Jews in Liverpool', *Transactions of the Historic Society of Lancashire and Cheshire* **LI**, 45–84

Burke, T A 1910 *The Catholic History of Liverpool.* Liverpool: Tinling & Co

Gibberd, Frederick 1968 *The Metropolitan Cathedral of Christ the King, Liverpool.* London: Architectural Press

Jones, R Merfyn and Rees, D Ben 1984 *The Liverpool Welsh and their Religion. Two Centuries of Welsh Calvinistic Methodism.* Liverpool: Modern Welsh Publications

Kadish, Sharman 2006 *Jewish Heritage in England: An Architectural Guide.* Swindon: English Heritage

Kennerley, Peter 1991 *The Building of Liverpool Cathedral.* Preston: Carnegie Publishing

Lewis, David 2001 *The Churches of Liverpool.* Liverpool: Bluecoat Press

Picton, J A 1875 *Memorials of Liverpool: Historical and Topographical,* 2 edn, 2 vols. London: Longmans, Green

Picton, J A 1883 *Selections from the Municipal Archives and Records from the 13th to the 17th Century.* Liverpool

Pollard, Richard and Pevsner, Nikolaus 2006 *The Buildings of England: Lancashire: Liverpool and the South-West.* New Haven and London: Yale University Press

Sharples, Joseph 2004 *Pevsner Architectural Guides: Liverpool.* New Haven and London: Yale University Press

Thom, T 1850 'On the scotch kirks and congregations in Liverpool, being a brief sketch of their rise and progress', *Transactions of the Historic Society of Lancashire and Cheshire* **II**, 69–84, 229–31

Troughton, T 1810 *The History of Liverpool.* London and Liverpool

Liverpool titles in the Informed Conservation series

Building a Better Society: Liverpool's historic institutional buildings.
Colum Giles, 2008. Product code 51332,
ISBN 9781873592908

Built on Commerce: Liverpool's central business district.
Joseph Sharples and John Stonard, 2008. Product code 51331,
ISBN 9781905624348

Ordinary Landscapes, Special Places: Anfield, Breckfield and the growth of Liverpool's suburbs.
Adam Menuge, 2008. Product code 51343,
ISBN 9781873592892

Places of Health and Amusement: Liverpool's historic parks and gardens.
Katy Layton-Jones and Robert Lee, 2008. Product code 51333,
ISBN 9781873592915

Religion and Place: Liverpool's historic places of worship.
Sarah Brown and Peter de Figueiredo, 2008. Product code 51334, ISBN 9781873592885

Storehouses of Empire: Liverpool's historic warehouses.
Colum Giles and Bob Hawkins, 2004. Product code 50920,
ISBN 9781873592809

Other titles in this series

Behind the Veneer: The South Shoreditch furniture trade and its buildings.
Joanna Smith and Ray Rogers, 2006. Product code 51204,
ISBN 9781873592960

The Birmingham Jewellery Quarter: An introduction and guide.
John Cattell and Bob Hawkins, 2000. Product code 50205,
ISBN 9781850747772

Bridport and West Bay: The buildings of the flax and hemp industry.
Mike Williams, 2006. Product code 51167,
ISBN 9781873592861

Built to Last? The buildings of the Northamptonshire boot and shoe industry.
Kathryn A Morrison with Ann Bond, 2004. Product code 50921, ISBN 9781873592793

Gateshead: Architecture in a changing English urban landscape.
Simon Taylor and David Lovie, 2004. Product code 52000,
ISBN 9781873592762

Manchester's Northern Quarter.
Simon Taylor and Julian Holder, 2008. Product code 50946,
ISBN 9781873592847

Manchester: The warehouse legacy – An introduction and guide.
Simon Taylor, Malcolm Cooper and P S Barnwell, 2002.
Product code 50668,
ISBN 9781873592670

Margate's Seaside Heritage.
Nigel Barker, Allan Brodie, Nick Dermott, Lucy Jessop and Gary Winter, 2007. Product code 51335,
ISBN 9781905624669

Newcastle's Grainger Town: An urban renaissance.
Fiona Cullen and David Lovie, 2003. Product code 50811,
ISBN 9781873592779

'One Great Workshop': The buildings of the Sheffield metal trades.
Nicola Wray, Bob Hawkins and Colum Giles, 2001. Product code 50214, ISBN 9781873592663

Religion and Place in Leeds.
John Minnis with Trevor Mitchell, 2007. Product code 51337,
ISBN 9781905624485

Stourport-on-Severn: Pioneer town of the canal age.
Colum Giles, Keith Falconer, Barry Jones and Michael Taylor, 2007. Product code 51290, ISBN 9781905624362

Weymouth's Seaside Heritage.
Allan Brodie, Colin Ellis, David Stuart and Gary Winter, 2008.
Product code 51429, ISBN 9781848020085

£7.99 each (plus postage and packing)
To order
Tel: EH Sales 01761 452966
Email: ehsales@gillards.com
Online bookshop: www.english-heritage.org.uk

Buildings of all
Denominations, 1905

Key

■ Anglican church

● Roman Catholic church

△ Building of other denomination

Main area of study

Cemetery

Public open space

[This map is based
upon Ordnance
Survey material with
the permission of
Ordnance Survey on
behalf of the
Controller of Her
Majesty's Stationery
Office © Crown
Copyright.
Unauthorised
reproduction infringes
Crown Copyright and
may lead to
prosecution or
criminal proceedings.
English Heritage
100019088.2008]

0   1 km

0   1 mile

Principal places of worship surviving or in use 2005

1   St Monica's, Bootle
2   St Winefride's, Bootle
3   St Mary's, Walton
4   Stuart Road Baptist Church
5   St Richard's, Bootle
6   St Francis de la Sales', Bootle
7   St Lawrence's, Westminster Close
8   County Methodist Church, Walton Road
9   Spellow Road Church (Independent)
10 St Luke's, Goodison Road
11 Westminster Road Congregational Chapel, Kirkdale
12 Liverpool Free Presbyterian Church, Spellow Lane
13 North Zion Independent Methodist Chapel, Tetlow Street, Kirkdale
14 St John the Evangelist's, Kirkdale
15 St Athanasius', Fountains Road, Kirkdale
16 Stanley Park Church, Walton Lane, Kirkdale
17 Chadwick Mount United Reformed Church, St Domingo Road, Everton
18 St Columba's, Pinehurst Road, Anfield
19 St Matthew's, Queen's Drive, Clubmoor
20 St Andrew's, Queen's Drive, Clubmoor
21 Temple of Praise, Anfield
22 Oakfield Methodist Church, Oakfield Road, Anfield
23 All Saints', Oakfield Road, Anfield
24 Richmond Baptist Church, Breck Road, Everton
25 Holy Trinity, Breck Lane
26 St Margaret's, Belmont Road
27 St Alban's (former), Athol Street
28 St Sylvester's, Silvester Street
29 Silvester Street Presbyterian Church
30 St Anthony's of Egypt, Scotland Road
31 St Polycarp's (former), Netherfield Road North, Everton
32 St George's, Heyworth Street, Everton
33 St Peter's, Sackville Street, Everton
34 Our Lady of Reconciliation de la Salette, Eldon Street, Vauxhall
35 Hill O'Zion Chapel, Netherfield Road South, Everton
36 Franciscan Friary Church of St Mary of the Angels (former), Fox Street
37 St Francis Xavier's, Salisbury Street
38 Particular Baptist Chapel (former), Shaw Street
39 Holy Cross, Great Crosshall Street
40 Our Lady and St Nicholas's, Chapel Street
41 Sacred Heart, Hall Lane
42 St Mary's, Edge Hill
43 Kensington Baptist Church (former)
44 Christ Church, Kensington

45 St Cyprian's, Durning Road, Edge Hill
46 Methodist Chapel, Toft Street
47 Shree Radha Krishna Mandir and Hindu Cultural Organisation, Edge Lane
48 St Philip's, Sheil Road
49 St John the Divine's, Holly Road, Fairfield
50 St Sebastian's, Lockerby Road, Fairfield
51 St John the Baptist's, Tuebrook
52 St Cecilia's, Tuebrook
53 St Anne's, Cheadle Avenue, Stanley
54 St Paul's, Derby Lane, Stoneycroft
55 Stoneycroft Wesleyan Chapel
56 St Oswald's King and Martyr, Old Swan
57 All Saints', Broadgreen Road, Stoneycroft
58 Gustav Adolfs Kyrka, Park Lane
59 St Michael's in the City, Upper Pitt Street
60 St Vincent de Paul's, St James' Street
61 Great George Street Congregational Chapel (former)
62 St Peter's (former), Seel Street
63 St Luke's (former), St Luke's Place
64 Methodist Central Hall, Renshaw Street
65 St Andrew's Scottish Presbyterian Church (former), Rodney Street
66 Third Church of Christ Scientist, Upper Parliament Street
67 St Bride's, Percy Street
68 St Philip Neri's, Catherine Street
69 German Church, Bedford Street North
70 Welsh Calvinist Methodist Church (former), Chatham Street
71 St Mary's, Overbury Street, Edge Hill
72 St Catherine's (former), Tunnel Road, Edge Hill
73 St James's, St James Place, Toxteth
74 St Patrick's, Park Place, Toxteth
75 Greek Orthodox Church of St Nicholas, Berkeley Street
76 St Margaret's of Antioch, Princes Road
77 Old Hebrew Congregation Synagogue, Princes Road
78 Welsh Presbyterian Church (former), Princes Road
79 Al-Rahma Mosque, Hatherley Street, Toxteth
80 Princes Park Methodist Church
81 Our Lady of Lourdes and St Bernard's, Toxteth
82 St Clement's, Beaumont Street
83 St Deniol's, Upper Parliament Street
84 St Dunstan's, Earle Road, Edge Hill
85 St Hugh's of Lincoln, Earle Road, Edge Hill
86 St Bridget's, Bagot Road, Wavertree
87 St Thomas', Ashfield, Wavertree
88 Sikh Gurdwara and Community Centre
89 St Mary's, North Drive, Wavertree

90 Our Lady of Good Help, Chestnut Grove, Wavertree
91 Congregational Church, Hunter's Lane, Wavertree
92 Progressive Synagogue, Wavertree
93 Holy Trinity, Church Road, Wavertree
94 St Stephen's United Reformed Church, Woolton Road
95 Christ the King, Queen's Drive
96 Toxteth Baptist Tabernacle, Park Place
97 St Malachy's, Beaufort Street, Toxteth
98 St Gabriel's, Beaufort Street, Toxteth
99 Park Street Church (former music hall), Beaumont Street, Toxteth
100 St Cleophas', Beresford Road, Toxteth
101 Wellington Road Methodist Church (former)
102 St Peter's Methodist Church, High Park Street, Toxteth
103 Our Lady of Mount Carmel, High Park Street, Toxteth
104 Gospel Hall, David Street, Toxteth
105 St Philemon's, Princes Park
106 Belvidere Road Independent Baptist Church, Princes Park
107 Presbyterian Chapel (former), Princes Park
108 Kingdom Hall of Jehovah's Witnesses, Princes Park
109 Ancient Chapel of Toxteth
110 Christ Church, Sefton Park
111 St Bede's, Hartington Road, Toxteth
112 St Agnes's, Ullet Road, Toxteth
113 Ullet Road Unitarian Church, Toxteth
114 St Clare's, Arundel Avenue, Sefton Park
115 New Hebrew Congretation Synagogue, Greenbank Drive, Sefton Park
116 Liverpool Mosque and Islamic Institute, Cramond Avenue
117 Heathfield Road Welsh Presbyterian Chapel, Smithdown Place
118 St Austin's, Aigburth
119 St Michael's in the Hamlet
120 St Charles Borromeo's, Aigburth Road
121 St Thomas More's, Rundle Road, Aigburth
122 Aigburth Methodist Church, Aigburth Road
123 St Anne's, Aigburth
124 St Christopher's, Lorenzo Drive, Norris Green
125 Rankin Presbyterian Church, Lorenzo Drive, Norris Green
126 Norris Green Baptist Church, Parthenon Drive and Utting Avenue
127 St Teresa's of the Child Jesus, Utting Avenue, Norris Green
128 Christ Church, Norris Green